THE PLOT TWIST IS YOU

& OTHER TRUTHS ABOUT WRITING THE COLLEGE ESSAY

Ava Mariya Gencheva

Copyright © 2025 Ava Mariya Gencheva

All rights reserved.

No part of this publication may be reproduced, stored in a retrieval system, or transmitted in any form or by any means—electronic, mechanical, photocopying, recording, or otherwise—without prior written permission of the publisher, except in the case of brief quotations embodied in critical reviews and certain other noncommercial uses permitted by copyright law.

Published in the United States of America by:

VoicED Press

San Francisco, CA

www.voicedacademy.com

ISBN: 979-8-9872904-5-3

Cover and interior design by David Provolo

Library of Congress Control Number: Applied for

First Edition: 2025

Printed in the United States of America

I am deeply grateful to my students, whose curiosity and determination inspire me to keep learning alongside them. Each story you share reminds me why this work matters and why every voice deserves to be heard. To the parents who have entrusted me with their most precious gift, your children, thank you for your trust, partnership, and belief in the journey we undertake together.

To my husband, whose steady encouragement has been my anchor through every chapter, and to my two children, who have given me life's greatest honor, the privilege of being called Mom, you are my truest plot twists, the ones who have changed my life in the most extraordinary ways.

This book is as much yours as it is mine, because in every story, just like in life, the plot twist is always you.

CONTENTS

INTRODUCTION 9
From Crisis to Clarity: Because the Right Words Change Everything

CHAPTER 1 13
Successful Strategy Beats Good Luck in the Long Run

CHAPTER 2 19
The Plot Twist Is You

CHAPTER 3 25
The Recipe for a Real Essay: Cook It Slowly

CHAPTER 4 29
What Admissions Officers Look For

CHAPTER 5 35
Dear Admissions Officer, Prepare to Be Dazzled

CHAPTER 6 41
Your Essay's Backbone: Building a Draft That Holds Up

CHAPTER 7 . . . . **47**
From Scattered to Strategic: Organizing Your Way In

CHAPTER 8 . . . . **55**
Can't Pick a Prompt? You're Not Alone; Here's What to Do

CHAPTER 9 . . . . **61**
How to Start: It's All About You (in 650 Words)

CHAPTER 10 . . . . **67**
Breaking Down a Prompt Word by Word and
Reading Between the Lines

CHAPTER 11 . . . . **71**
Prewriting and Brainstorming Like a Pro

CHAPTER 12 . . . . **79**
Find Your Focus and Sharpen Your Story:
The Formula for a Standout Essay

CHAPTER 13 . . . . **85**
Learning Storytelling from Disney

CHAPTER 14.........................**91**
Where the Rubber Meets the Road: Examples
of Successful Personal Statements

CHAPTER 15.........................**117**
School-Specific Essays: How to Approach
the "Why Us?" Essay

CHAPTER 16.........................**141**
Elevate Your Style: Mastering the Braided Essay

CHAPTER 17.........................**151**
Your Essay Is an Invitation

CHAPTER 18.........................**155**
Avoiding the Trap of Overemphasizing Accomplishments

CHAPTER 19.........................**161**
Digging for Gold: Memorable Writing Balances
Logic and Emotion

CHAPTER 20.........................**175**
Words Matter: Visual Language

CHAPTER 21..................................**181**
Make Me Feel It: The Science Behind Showing, Not Telling

CHAPTER 22..................................**187**
What Is a Personality Score?

CHAPTER 23..................................**193**
Demonstrating Interest from the Start

CHAPTER 24..................................**195**
Tilt the Odds

ABOUT THE AUTHOR........................**198**

ADMISSIBILITY CHECKLIST.................**200**

ADMISSIBILITY APPENDIX:.................**203**
Your Final Plot Twist

ACKNOWLEDGMENTS.......................**206**

INTRODUCTION

From Crisis to Clarity: Because the Right Words Change Everything

> "THE DIFFERENCE BETWEEN THE RIGHT WORD AND THE ALMOST RIGHT WORD IS THE DIFFERENCE BETWEEN LIGHTNING AND A LIGHTNING BUG."
> — MARK TWAIN

was inspired to write this book when one of my students handed me what he thought was a finished personal statement. The prompt asked him to reflect on leadership. His essay, 700 words long, was polished and grammatically correct. In two minutes,

I knew it wasn't his voice. It read like a résumé disguised as a short story, impressive on the surface but lacking life.

He had spent weeks refining what he believed admissions officers wanted to hear, not realizing that his "perfect" essay made him sound like everyone else. Worse, it masked his actual strengths. And this wasn't an isolated case. I have worked as a college counselor and educational coach for over twenty years, helping students from diverse backgrounds, including first-generation, high-achieving, undecided, artistic, STEM-focused, and everything in between. I've seen this scenario happen hundreds of times. College essays fall apart not from lack of effort but from misdirected effort. Students are taught to perform, not to reflect. To produce, not to reveal. And when the time comes to write something personal, most have no idea how to start.

This book is my response. It's a guide to clarity over performance and process over panic. It's for every student whose voice got lost in a sea of bullet points and buzzwords, and who wants it back.

The student essays in this book come from my experience working with students in California, one of the most competitive and high-pressure college admissions environments in the country. But that's exactly why they're valuable to study. These students succeeded not because they had perfect résumés, but because they learned how to tell their stories in a clear and emotionally compelling way. These storytelling techniques helped students stand out in some of the most competitive applicant pools, where GPAs and test scores were nearly indistinguishable.

Before I begin introducing some of these helpful writing techniques, I would like to assure you, the reader, of my sincere efforts to provide a clear and helpful narration of writing and editing strategies, and in turn, ask you to put your sincere efforts into internalizing and applying these to your work.

INTRODUCTION

I've heard many questions and concerns over the years of working with students, helping them gain admission to their desired colleges and universities:

- How do I decide which colleges to add to my list? I don't even understand the differences between Common and Coalition applications.
- What is the real cost of attendance, and how do I navigate FAFSA?
- My parents want me to apply to Stanford and other highly competitive schools, but I don't know much about their admissions criteria, which stresses me out.
- My high school counselors don't really know me, and it takes months to get replies to my emails.
- What matters more: my AP tests or my SAT and ACT scores? Is test-optional still a thing?
- I don't have time for things I enjoy, but all I hear is that my "passion" matters most. How do I find my passion when I am so busy keeping up with deadlines, school, and extracurricular activities?
- How do colleges evaluate students, and how important is my personal statement? Should I include my extracurricular activities in it?
- The college application asks for so much from me; I feel like I'm decoding a foreign language.
- I'm not confident in my writing skills, so how can I craft compelling and authentic personal statements or supplemental essays that speak about my experiences?
- The pressure to stand out by sharing my experiences is making me more frustrated and anxious than ever.

Here, we will examine the challenge that looms over every student when putting together the college application, specifically the essay portion.

However, before we begin with the strategies of excellent writing, we need to pause and take a step back. Writing your statement isn't just about putting words on a page; it's about understanding the power behind those words.

This is where actual writing begins: You choose to tell about yourself, not only about your past, but also about a powerful force that can shape your future.

Think of this writing process not as a boring task or homework that will earn you a grade, but as crafting the first chapter of your life using words to connect with others.

CHAPTER 1

Successful Strategy Beats Good Luck in the Long Run

THE ABILITY TO SHIFT PERSPECTIVES TURNS CONFUSION INTO CLARITY AND SETBACKS INTO STORIES.

Most people focus on the outcome when starting a new project. But I once saw an interview with a gambler named Mikki Mase. I found his strategies to be unique and insightful, even though at first glance, they seemed completely unrelated to the writing process. His controversial approach led to success at the table, and there was definitely something to learn from it.

He shared that his consistent wins come from never betting like everyone else. While others stare at the spinning roulette wheel, Mase keeps his eyes lowered, scanning the floor.

In the interview, he described walking into a casino and immediately noticing that the carpet beneath one of the roulette tables was subtly worn down on one side. I've never gambled, but I was struck by his instinct. He noticed what most people miss in the noise and chaos of the room: years of players leaning forward from the same spot had unknowingly created a slight tilt. That tiny shift was enough to make the ball fall toward one side more often.

Mase didn't win by luck but by the power of his observation.

For him, it wasn't fate or chance but physics and leverage.

I don't support gambling, and ironically, neither does Mase. But I respect the mindset behind it. Systems, even those made to seem random, have patterns. They show signs. Those who succeed aren't always the loudest or most aggressive; often, they're the ones who watch and analyze. The core idea of this chapter is paying attention to the lean at the table rather than the ball in motion.

Now, think of college admissions. Most people obsess over the well-known wheel: GPA, test scores, clubs, and leadership. It looks like this is what the game is about, but in reality, it's just the surface. The tilt, the leverage, lives somewhere else. Somewhere beneath. Most students only go through this process once, and by the time they realize where they stand, the results are out, and the damage is done. That's why strategy matters. And that's why having someone who's walked the room before matters more than people admit. I have never seen a championship athlete, a startup founder, or even a jackpot winner succeed alone. The idea of the lone genius is a myth. Behind every outlier, there's a strategy and often, competent guidance in the form of a coach, a book, or a well-wisher.

Mase's gift was observation. But what happens when observation meets math? That's where Ed Thorp comes in. Thorp was a mathematics professor at UCLA who didn't just observe the table; he calculated its mechanics. He wrote *Beat the Dealer*, the first book to break down how card-counting worked in blackjack and turned Vegas on its head. Later, he brought the same statistical vision to Wall Street and built one of the earliest quantitative hedge funds.

"You don't need to cheat the system if you can see its pattern," he once said. And that's it. That's the key.

Systems look random until you step back far enough to see how they're built. Admissions, like blackjack, isn't just about what's on the surface. Every college has patterns: college majors they can't fill, zip codes they want to accept for representation, personalities they crave, and music groups or athletic teams they need the numbers for. If you can figure out what a school's culture and demands are before you apply, you don't just check boxes on the application; you develop a profile that fulfills a specific need.

There are other tells, too. Did you know that colleges track demonstrated interest? They log how many times you open their emails, attend their virtual tours, and engage with their social media. This isn't a romantic meritocracy. It's a data-driven ecosystem. And yes, it's imperfect. But if you're paying attention, those imperfections are where the light gets in.

And what if, like Charlie Munger—Warren Buffett's longtime partner and one of the most successful investors of the twentieth and early twenty-first centuries, who defied investment trends to build a personal fortune of over $100 billion—you stop approaching the problem head-on and instead invert it? Munger, a man of solid logic and big-picture thinking, constructed a comprehensive framework of mental models that drew upon fields such as psychology, biology, engineering, and history, which helped him become one of the most successful entrepreneurs and philanthropists of our time. He didn't believe in just solving problems; he believed in flipping them upside down. "Invert, always invert," he said. In other words, don't ask what a college wants from you. Ask what problem they're trying to solve and how you might be their unexpected answer. Study the research their graduating students publish, pay attention to the school's mission statement, and read between the lines of what is listed on their website.

These thinkers share a common perspective: They study the patterns and forge their own path.

Another example is a name you've likely never heard of: Temple Grandin. She reengineered the cattle industry not through machinery but through empathy. She didn't see hallways and fences; she saw motion, fear, bottlenecks, and discomfort where the animals lived. Her autistic brain allowed her to visualize flow in ways others couldn't. She wasn't trained to think like this; she simply did. The result? She pioneered and implemented massive changes with a new system of calming animals and preventing them from being hurt when handled, using her invention known as the "hug machine."

Isn't that precisely what colleges claim to look for? Not another perfect applicant, but someone who sees differently, thinks differently, brings an angle others don't. And yet, many students suppress their unique ways of seeing, out of fear that they won't be understood. Grandin teaches the opposite: Different isn't broken, it is an insight not yet understood.

Then there's Apollo Robbins, the pickpocket turned cognitive magician. Robbins doesn't steal; he studies how human attention works. He knows where people will and won't look. That's his trick. It works not because he's faster, but because he's smarter about what people ignore.

Imagine your essay is a performance. What does your reader expect? A story of adversity? A declaration of passion? Good. Now disrupt it. Flip it. Begin in the middle. End with the beginning, flip it on its head, not to be clever, but to be unforgettable. That's what Charlie Munger would do; that is also Robbins's move.

In every one of these examples, from gamblers to grandmasters, from scientists to social engineers, we see one thread: Those who succeed aren't the ones who try to be better; they're the ones who think deeper.

Even in everyday systems, the cracks are visible. One student discovered that his college's course registration system consistently crashed at 3:07 p.m. on registration day. Submitting too early wasn't an option; the portal only accepted entries within a specific window, and early submissions were flagged or blocked by the system. But if you waited too long, the system would crash, or classes would appear full due to automated overbooking precautions. So, he timed the process and submitted his form at 3:06 p.m. every time. He never got waitlisted. That's not hacking; he was strategically precise within a flawed, rule-based system. That's the power of precision observation.

And speaking of precision, consider the chess champion Magnus Carlsen. He doesn't play the game everyone else prepares for. He plays against the opponent. While others memorize openings, Magnus senses hesitation. "I don't look for the best move," he says. "I look for the move that makes my opponent uncomfortable."

Admissions is no different. The application isn't about perfection. It's about disruption. You don't need to impress, but you need to be remembered by how moving your story is. When you impress, you trigger the orbitofrontal cortex, a region in the brain that evaluates and expects outcomes. However, when your work is moving and heartfelt, the amygdala and anterior cingulate cortex work together to activate strong emotional responses, leading to a heightened feeling of elation.

So, read the room. Don't just answer the prompt but use the prompt to tell your story and infuse it with emotion. Flip the frame.

Because every system, no matter how fortified, has a flaw. Every gate has a hinge, and sometimes, all it takes is a new angle, a question inverted, a bet placed just before the spin, or an observant student to find a new way in.

That's your move.

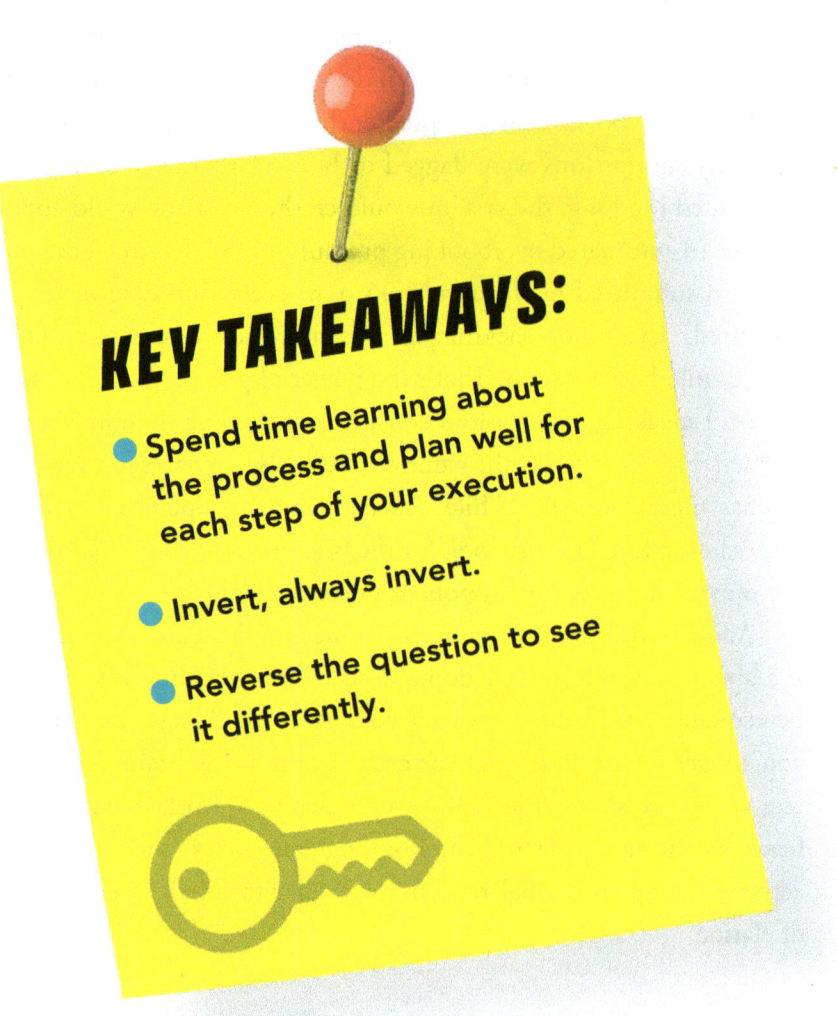

KEY TAKEAWAYS:
- Spend time learning about the process and plan well for each step of your execution.
- Invert, always invert.
- Reverse the question to see it differently.

CHAPTER 2

The Plot Twist Is You

> *IF YOU DON'T SHAPE YOUR STORY, THE READER'S IMAGINATION WILL DO IT FOR YOU, AND YOU MAY NOT LIKE THE VERSION IT TELLS.*

The plot twist is you, the writer. That's a simple truth I realized one day while desperately trying to craft a funny hook for a speech. My humor tends toward dark, and my writing is rarely laugh-out-loud funny, so I spent days analyzing jokes just to understand how they work. It wasn't until I googled "What is a joke?" that it clicked: Every joke needs two elements, a premise and a twist. The setup builds an expectation, and the twist breaks it. That's where the punchline lives. And it struck me: The same rhythm, the same tension, the same surprise exist in all great writing. A good story isn't born in the setup; it's born in the turn. And when you write about yourself, that turning point—the insight, the shift, the contradiction—is where the story begins. That's why, in the best essays, you are the plot twist: the part no one saw coming.

That surprise moment isn't just for effect; it is a reminder that perception shapes reality without replacing it. When you reveal yourself at the precipice of expectation, you don't just tell your story, but you change how it's received. Understanding this interplay between the facts you present and the lens through which they're viewed is crucial not only for a standout college application but also for every challenge you'll face in life.

Once you grasp this, how a single line can shift an admissions officer's whole impression, you'll see it play out every day: in convincing a skeptical teacher, negotiating a job offer, even pitching a startup idea.

Your immediate application of this truth begins with preparing for college and writing your personal statement.

You might have heard the saying "A is A," a principle rooted in Aristotelian logic and later popularized by the Russian-born American philosopher and author Ayn Rand's philosophy of objectivism, which affirms that reality is objective, and facts are unchanging. And yes, "A" is still "A." Objective truth exists. However, in most human matters, especially in how people judge one another, perception becomes nine-tenths of what others act upon.

When it comes to your college application, how you present yourself and the first impression you create about your intellect and personality will be how your application is judged and scored. Think of this as your public relations moment and ultimate claim to authority.

Which brings us to Edward Bernays, the man credited with inventing modern public relations. Bernays was more than a PR agent; he was a pioneer in the psychological manipulation of public perception. He was Sigmund Freud's nephew, and he used psychological ideas from Freud to develop methods that influenced public opinion and consumer behavior on a mass scale. Bernays is the mind behind the infamous Torches of Freedom campaign that encouraged women to smoke cigarettes as a symbol of liberation. He's the reason why flavored bacon became popular and why the Department of War rebranded itself as the Department of Defense. His obituary described him as the father of public relations, and although his techniques were effective, they were often manipulative.

Why is this relevant to you?

Because your personal statement, your college essay, is your PR moment. **You are the brand.** Your words will frame how the admissions officer perceives you. And perception, as Bernays proved, drives action. So, you can insist that A is A, but unless others see it, feel it, or believe it, they'll judge you as if A is B.

Let's go deeper. When you write your college essay, you do more than tell a story; you build a frame, a psychological and storytelling structure that shapes how the reader interprets and emotionally connects with the story. Frames are not optional; the human brain demands them. Every reader, including your admissions officer, will instinctively and immediately form mental pictures, emotions, and judgments based on the frame you create. They can't help it. The brain hates loose data. It snaps every word you write into a narrative, and that narrative becomes you in their mind.

This is where branding starts. You're not branding yourself with slogans or claims. Instead, you're shaping your brand through the stories you tell and how you tell them. Your words set the framework and direct the reader's focus. If your framework is clear—like "I am resilient and not afraid of trial and error," "I am curious and have self-studied much of my calculus," or "I create solutions when others freeze"—every detail you include becomes evidence. If your framework is jumbled or your story contradicts your intent, the reader's mind fills the gaps, often against you. You can't control how they frame you, only how you present yourself.

Here's what happens when you get it wrong: You write about your hardships, but focus so much on the difficulty that the reader frames you as overwhelmed. You discuss leadership, but your story primarily focuses on issues with your team. You describe yourself as passionate, but the essay comes across as somewhat flat. Subliminally, the reader's mind says: "Nice student, but maybe not ready." You never said that, but your frame did.

Here's what happens when you get it right: You write about a challenge, but the energy is on how you moved through it, what you learned, and what you built next. Your words framed setbacks as pivot points. Your language shows momentum, curiosity, and growth. The reader's mind concludes, "This student is someone who finds a way forward. This student will thrive here." Again, you never said it outright. The frame you used conveyed it for you, and it stuck.

And here's a big one: the language that leaks unconscious bias. I've seen this even in well-meaning students. Last year, a student wrote extensively about working with individuals who are neurodivergent. She had good intentions, but the way she used certain words and phrases created a frame of pity rather than respect. The underlying implication, unintentionally, was that she saw the people she worked with as "less than." It took multiple sessions to help her rewrite the narrative, not because she needed to change the activity she did, but to help her display her fundamental values within her frame and shape the reader's perception.

The bottom line is that the human mind is a meaning-making machine. It reads between every line. When you choose your words carefully and structure your story with intent, you aren't just sharing facts; you are guiding perception, emotion, and memory. That's the real power of writing. You're not just telling them who you are. You are helping them feel it, believe it, and remember it.

Here are some reflection prompts for you:

1. How do I want to be remembered after someone reads my essay? (Write one sentence that captures the "frame" that shapes the reader's emotional response, and you want to be remembered by.)

2. Can I think of a time someone misunderstood my intent because of how I said or wrote something? (What was the difference between what you meant and what they heard?)

3. What does my current story (on paper or in my head) imply about me, even without saying it directly? Does it show curiosity? Resilience? Responsibility? Or does it lean toward doubt, blame (be careful of the blame game), or playing it safe? What emotions does it evoke? Admiration? Curiosity? Or confusion?

4. What words or phrases do I tend to use that might accidentally create a frame I don't want? (Hint: Look for overuse of passive voice, vague adjectives, or pity-based framing.)

5. What role would Edward Bernays say I'm applying for if he read my essay? (Am I being a historian, a visionary, a problem-solver? And which role am I unintentionally casting myself in?)

KEY TAKEAWAYS:

- Admissions officers look at your narrative patterns:
  - This student overcomes obstacles with clarity.
  - This student is interesting, but their story feels flat.
  - This student claims to be passionate, but I don't feel it.

- You don't control their assumptions, but you get to guide what they assume by the story you tell and the words you choose.

- Framing your story with vivid language isn't manipulation; it's intention. It's the difference between being misunderstood and being unforgettable.

CHAPTER 3

The Recipe for a Real Essay: Cook It Slowly

> START WRITING BEFORE YOU'RE READY. CLARITY COMES THROUGH THE ACT OF EXPRESSION, NOT BEFORE IT.

College essay writing is a process, and to give this process the care and attention it deserves, we need to choose our words carefully. You are asked to follow the steps outlined in this book because words have meaning; overlooking this advice can cost you time and, more importantly, the positive results you're aiming for.

Following the writing process involves letting your essay ferment, develop, and evolve. Time will test your written words and help *you* determine their value. I learned this from my college professors, but it remained a theory until I applied it myself, receiving full confirmation from many great storytellers. I would like to quote one such master director and storyteller to inspire you to explore more written works outside of your high school curriculum.

In one of his interviews, Steven Spielberg, known not only for his iconic films but also for his writing and story development in works like *E.T. the Extra-Terrestrial*, *Poltergeist*, *A.I. Artificial Intelligence*, and the original stories for *Jaws*, *Jurassic Park*, and *Raiders of the Lost Ark*, was asked how he generates ideas and discerns which ones will make great stories. He said, "All good ideas start as bad ideas; that's why it takes so long." He writes down ideas to see if they still make sense after a long time has passed. Usually, a good idea and a strong plot will grab your attention regardless of how much time passes. The test of time is like no other. One of Spielberg's strategies is revisiting his ideas over time to see if they still resonate with him. In his advice to writers and directors, he emphasizes the significance of staying devoted to the original idea and trusting the creative process. This includes revisiting past concepts and seeing them from different angles. This method helps determine whether an idea maintains its strength and relevance over time.

Spielberg's technique of jotting down ideas and allowing them to sit before revisiting them to ensure they still hold the same impact is an excellent method used by filmmakers and writers. His approach to directing how the story is emotionally and visually framed has made him a master architect of the story's experience. This approach enables him to assess the durability and potential of his ideas over time. If an idea continues to resonate with you after a while, it's likely a strong one deserving of pursuit. Throughout this book, I advise adopting this method for writing your personal statement essay.

In many ways, writing your personal statement is like creating a movie. You need to balance the content and ideas with the writing process. Focusing on the process means following a plan to produce a high-quality result. The word "essay" originally meant "to test" or "try out." Therefore, your college essay should tell a story about you by highlighting your personality, interests, and how you handle challenges. It gives people a sense of who you are. Advanced placement classes, SAT scores, and grades are just "threshold" elements to top colleges, so many elite universities enjoy rejecting perfect scores. One poorly written essay can easily undermine all your impressive numbers.

KEY TAKEAWAYS:

- Good writing takes time to evolve, and adding new ideas is part of the process. Rushing leads to flat, uninspired writing.

- Let time test your writing: You won't know if your essay works until you revisit it after a few days, even weeks.

CHAPTER 4

What Admissions Officers Look For

> "WE CAN SPOT A POLISHED RÉSUMÉ FROM A MILE AWAY. BUT A THOUGHTFUL ESSAY? THAT MAKES US NOT JUST READ BUT RELATE TO THE HUMAN."
> — ADMISSIONS OFFICER, NORTHEASTERN UNIVERSITY

Do admissions officers read all essays?

Yes, they do. This is the only way for them to learn about the person beyond grades and accolades. For you, the essay is an opportunity to tell your story in your voice. Stories define us! Our history and turning points show who we are becoming; this is your chance to shine or make a big mistake. Reading your writing lets the reader step into your thoughts and desires. The essay is an X-ray of your thought process and intellect. That may sound frightening, but it's the truth.

The personal statement has been part of college applications since the 1920s. It was introduced to help admissions officers better understand the applicant's personality, and today, in many ways, it has also become a substitute for the interview. Over the last few decades, the role of the personal statement has undergone significant changes as standardized tests have become less popular and grade inflation has emerged as a growing concern. The personal statement and college-specific supplemental essays have become increasingly important in the admissions process in recent years. Additionally, the Common Application and the Coalition Application have enabled students to apply to twenty colleges simultaneously, increasing competition as more students apply to more schools each year with a single click. As a result, admissions officers must rely on factors such as the essay to differentiate among groups of students whose grades and test scores are very similar. Most students believe that the colleges and the college admissions officers judge only the students' writing skills, but the written portion of the application reveals way more than just the quality of your writing.

The terms "holistic admissions" and "personality score" are often used on college websites, but they can add to the confusion surrounding the admission process and the role of the personal statement. "Holistic admissions" means the college considers *the whole applicant,* beyond just grades and test scores. This includes extracurricular activities, background, leadership, service, and, yes, the personal statement. "Personality score," on the other hand, is often an informal label used during admissions review to evaluate intangible traits, such as passion, grit, empathy, originality, and intellectual curiosity, based on the personal statement, supplemental essays, letters of recommendation, and interviews. Neither is entirely objective, and that's exactly why the personal statement, a 650-word essay, matters so much. Here is what the essay reveals about you:

Your time management. Can you meet the deadline for the applications and write a meaningful and well-written essay(s)?

Your analytical skills. Can you utilize self-reflection and authenticity? How do you interpret and analyze your life and your roots?

Your logical thinking. Can you organize and structure your thoughts and ideas logically?

Your academic viability. What is your command of English grammar, mechanics, and vocabulary?

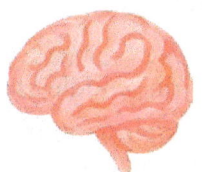

Your ability to self-reflect is one of the most critical aspects of your personality. Can you answer the questions clearly and in a personable manner?

Your essay can also explain your identity, family history, and, most importantly, your grades and test scores, especially if they fall below the median reported by the school(s) you're applying to. If this is the case, you'll need something on your application that makes you stand out from the crowd and helps compensate for any shortcomings. An excellent essay can do just that, within reason. Many competitive colleges in the country use a rating system that separates academic achievement, GPA, and APs from your personal experiences by assigning a personality score after reading the 650-word personal statement and college-specific supplemental essays. Ultimately, both your academic and personality scores are taken into consideration. With an impressive personal story, you can improve your overall chances of acceptance.

When it's time for the admissions committee to vote, the officer assigned to your state—your regional officer, who has read your application and knows your high school context—presents your file. If they believe in you, they'll advocate for a yes vote, and their support can be the deciding factor.

Typically, students who benefit most from a strong personal statement are those in the middle range of grades. If you're applying to a school that admits students at or above a 4.0 GPA and your numbers are significantly lower, an essay likely won't help much. The numbers will be the determining factor unless you possess a unique talent in music, excel in competitive sports, or achieve remarkable accomplishments in some other field.

However, if you're in the middle range, a compelling personal statement can elevate your application from the rejected pile.

When Melissa applied to Northeastern, her 3.8 GPA placed her in the middle of the pack. But her personal statement about building a makeshift community garden during remote learning stood out. In vivid detail, she described negotiating plot space with local seniors, teaching classmates to compost, and overcoming a sudden frost that threatened their seedlings. The admissions officers included a handwritten note on Melissa's acceptance letter, stating that her story "jumped off the page," showcasing her leadership, creativity, and grit—all qualities that no GPA could fully capture. Melissa's garden essay transformed a good candidate into a good, admissible one.

KEY TAKEAWAYS:

- The admissions process is long and complicated, and a strong essay can flip the verdict in your favor.

- Your story reveals everything about you. (Let the word "everything" sink in.)

CHAPTER 5

Dear Admissions Officer, Prepare to Be Dazzled

"A CAPTIVATING ESSAY ISN'T JUST READ — IT'S REMEMBERED."
— COLLEGE ADMISSIONS READER

When we think of the college admissions committee, we might imagine a stuffy room full of people armed with stacks of applications, their bored, square faces so formal that even the dust bunnies in the corners are wearing ties. This vision can dampen your spirit. Instead of focusing on the audience, as every essay writing teacher might say, you should focus on yourself. Don't worry about how to attract and hold their attention; that problem isn't yours right now. You only need to concentrate on yourself and remember that your story is unique because you are unique. You don't need to stress about being original. Your originality is inherent, and you might compromise it by getting too stiff with worry about how you come across. It might help to imagine a bored bureaucrat whose mind craves innovation and yearns for the unexpected, suddenly sitting upright as your words leap off the page. Picture their faces lighting up, their hands waving your application like a victorious pirate brandishing treasure. "This one has spunk. They've invented a language spoken entirely in puns! Brilliant!"

It is not so much about the story but how it is told.

So, dare to dream, dare to dazzle, and who knows? You might just charm your way past the gates of academia with a well-placed pun or a dash of whimsy.

Many colleges hire a diverse team of readers, called admissions officers, who are responsible for reviewing applications, including your essays. There's no single profile that defines who reads your file: Some are former teachers, school counselors, alumni, or professionals with backgrounds in education, writing, or even business. They are all people like you and me from diverse backgrounds, young and old, conservative and liberal. Some large universities, such as the University of Texas at Austin, can have up to eighty such employees. In the case of the University of California system, the numbers go five times higher than that. A dean, or director of admissions, usually leads a team of assistant or associate directors. Some schools even hire faculty and interns, who might still be working toward their postgraduate degrees and are familiar with the school culture, to evaluate applicants. This might be your future professor reading your story and sizing you up.

Most, if not all, universities have an admissions representative responsible for a specific geographic area, which can include international regions if the school attracts many international students. These officers typically handle connections within their designated region. Before you even apply, you may be contacted by a representative from your area if you have expressed interest in visiting the school. Schools like Baylor University or Rice University often have an admissions representative meet with you the summer before the application process starts. These meetings aren't formal interviews, but they give the admissions representative a chance to get to know you early, which can influence how your application is later viewed.

These admissions representatives travel to their specific target areas to attend college fairs, conduct interviews, and speak at secondary schools. This is why you can reach out to them; they are available to applicants to answer questions and give a better idea of what the school they represent is like (especially if they are alumni).

When admissions applications are submitted, the committee's work goes into high gear. Some schools receive hundreds or even thousands of applications for each spot in the first-year class.

Believe me when I tell you that at the end of the day, Admissions finds it refreshing to discover students who love their families, schools, and friends, and care about issues you care about. Yet, they are looking for a reason to reject you.

Mini Glossary

Holistic admissions. An evaluation approach in which officers consider an applicant's complete profile—grades, test scores, essays, activities, background, and character—rather than relying solely on numerical metrics.

Personality score. An informal rubric used by some schools to quantify traits such as leadership, resilience, creativity, and empathy, as evidenced in essays and recommendations.

Supplemental essay. A college-specific writing prompt (beyond the main personal statement) that asks applicants to address particular programs (usually honors), college majors, clubs, or campus culture.

Common Application & Coalition Application. Centralized platforms that allow students to apply to multiple colleges with one core set of materials; supplemental questions still vary by institution.

Transcript "hook." A detail, such as a unique project, a way you overcame adversity, or an unusual passion, that an essay uses to capture an admissions reader's attention beyond GPAs and test scores.

Word count ceiling. The maximum number of words allowed for an essay; staying just under this limit demonstrates respect for guidelines and strong editing skills.

DEAR ADMISSIONS OFFICER, PREPARE TO BE DAZZLED

KEY TAKEAWAYS:

- Trying too hard to be original will make you just the opposite: mundane.

- Your main audience includes people of all ages and genders; there is no one-size-fits-all method.

CHAPTER 6

Your Essay's Backbone: Building a Draft That Holds Up

> THE ESSAY STRUCTURE IS NOT A CAGE — IT'S A FRAME. WITHOUT IT, THE STORY COLLAPSES UNDER ITS OWN WEIGHT.

Here's a common piece of advice for college essay writing: Your personal statement should sound like you. But what does that mean? You have a voice you use with your friends, another with your teachers, and yet another with your parents. Which one is right for your essay? To figure this out, your goal is to find the answer to *why you are writing about this topic*. Why does this matter to you? Why should it matter to anyone else? Until you figure that out, your story will be missing a heartbeat. If the only reason to write is to respond to a prompt, your *why* will not be strong enough to carry the plot. You will end up wandering through the narrative like I do when I am lost in a mall parking lot. Admissions officers can sense that confusion and lack of clarity, the way a chef can smell from far away if someone added the wrong spices to his signature sauce.

The kind of writing that reflects your voice will have the "I care about this stuff" factor. Your own voice, for your own reasons. If you're not there yet, stop, step back, and figure out where you lost your way. Once you understand your *why*, your voice will come naturally.

When I read a Stephen King story, I know it's his before I even see his name on the cover. The voice is his. The story and the characters are his. Shuffle his pages into a stack of strangers' work, and his voice would still stand out as King's. Take *The Shining*, for example, famous for its eerie setting, depicting the Overlook Hotel, an isolated old resort in the American Rockies, and a recovering alcoholic writer hoping for peace and a fresh start with his wife and son. Early on, King starts with an idiom:

"A closed mouth gathers no feet."

It's a sly line tucked into a tense conversation, dark humor amid dread, where two unfortunate souls and their ordinary, everyday lives coexist closely with magical, paranormal, and inexplicable events. That's pure King: horror that exists right alongside the everyday, with characters who sound like someone you actually know.

Now compare that to a writer most everyone has encountered in high school: F. Scott Fitzgerald's *The Great Gatsby*. His style couldn't be more different, yet it's just as unmistakable.

"So, we beat on, boats against the current, borne back ceaselessly into the past."

This voice is lyrical, nostalgic, and soothing. You could hand that line to someone who's read Gatsby once, years ago, and they'd still recognize it instantly.

And then there's Angie Thomas in *The Hate U Give*. She opens the novel with:

"I shouldn't have come to this party."

Short and punchy statement, and we're already in Starr's world, direct and full of tension. Thomas's voice addresses the reader as if sitting across from you, personal and authentic. King, Fitzgerald, and Thomas couldn't sound more different, but they all "own" their narratives. You can feel them in every line. That's what you're aiming for, not to sound like them, but to sound like you, in a way no one could mistake.

One of the easiest ways to discover the right voice for your essay is to keep a journal. This might seem like odd advice and unrelated to the primary task you must accomplish. But it is a great method for beginning your essay, for two important reasons. First, your journal will reflect your voice, allowing you to practice honing it. When writing your essay, you can use the journal as a reference for tone and word choices that convey your authentic voice. The second reason for keeping a journal is that it can be a great source of ideas. In it, you can write about what's important to you, your goals and aspirations, your values, and your take on everything from popular culture to current events. Your journal, coupled with the information you gather in your inventory (which we'll get to later in this chapter), is the perfect source of raw data to begin the essay writing process.

Journaling doesn't have to be an elaborate, time-consuming process. Take as little as five minutes a day to write about something personal. To journal effectively, you need to make it a routine, so the process needs to be as painless and straightforward as possible. Reflect on your daily habits and routines and adopt a journaling strategy that suits you best. You can write on paper, make journal entries on your computer, or keep a blog.

Pick a time and place to write in your journal each day. If you're writing on paper, get a small journal to carry with you everywhere you go. Therefore, when inspiration hits, you'll be ready. If you're typing, set aside a specific time to work at your computer. If that doesn't work, use the notes app on your phone, add a few bullet points, or speak into it. When the time comes for you to write your essays, you will be glad you did.

Beginning this way, Maya wrote one sentence each morning during summer break about her grandmother's recipes. Six weeks later, she included a cooking anecdote directly into her first draft, and that "flavor" detail earned her an acceptance letter with a merit scholarship.

YOUR ESSAY'S BACKBONE: BUILDING A DRAFT THAT HOLDS UP

KEY TAKEAWAYS:

- Spend five minutes a day capturing authentic thoughts; those raw entries become the bank you'll borrow from when starting to brainstorm and write your personal statement and college-specific essays.

- Sketch your story's frame (your main idea + structure) first, then layer in sensory details from your journal to bring it to life.

- Don't tell readers you're resilient; instead, show it by choosing moments from your journal that prove resilience in action.

CHAPTER 7

From Scattered to Strategic: Organizing Your Way In

> WRITING YOUR COLLEGE ESSAY WITHOUT UNDERSTANDING THE APPLICATION IS LIKE REHEARSING A MONOLOGUE BEFORE READING THE ENTIRE SCRIPT. IT MIGHT SOUND GOOD, BUT YOU'LL MISS THE ROLE ENTIRELY.

Now that you've created your story inventory by beginning to journal (from Chapter 6), let's explore how to fit those narratives into the Common App framework.

Start this planning at the end of your junior year and use a timeline to stay organized.

June: Journal, gather, and brainstorm ideas.

July: Outline Common App essay (the 650-word personal statement that is sent to *every* college you apply to through the Common Application).

August: Draft and solicit feedback on supplemental essays. These are the *college-specific* essays that are usually shorter (100–300 words) and vary by school.

Red flag: Avoid jumping to forced "big stories" that don't reflect your authentic voice.

I know from experience that you are already asking yourself: How can I make my essay more compelling? What stories should I include?

Let's begin with the Common Application and a common mistake I warn against. Many people start writing and filling out the application from the middle, focusing on the activities section first, jumping between sections, and entering information in disconnected bits without stepping back to ensure the application tells a clear, cohesive story of who they are. If your writing process is like skipping to dessert before tasting the entrée, you're not alone.

Think of it as eating lunch out of order: some main course, dessert, and salad. This backward order leads to confusion, a lack of perspective, and incomplete work. Instead, start by introducing yourself to the whole application structure. Take the wide-angle lens first to get the big picture and read between the lines.

You are not just filling out a simple application; you are creating a profile of yourself as a person with talents, thoughts, experiences, and aspirations. The Common Application is accepted by nearly 1,400 colleges and universities across the United States. Each college or university may require supplemental essays, sometimes as many as twelve, which can range from 350 to 750 words in length. Since many schools use similar prompts, it makes sense to start brainstorming your supplemental essays at the beginning of summer before senior year (but start journaling and collecting your ideas and experiences earlier) and to organize them by common themes and application deadlines. Each topic can reveal what the school values in a candidate, what the admissions officers review, and what to avoid discussing.

For example, a topic might expect you to evaluate a significant experience, achievement, risk you have taken, or ethical dilemma you have faced, and its impact on you. The last phrase is critical; whatever you choose to write about (the cause), you must show its impact upon you (the effect). Your experience need not be earth-shattering; keeping it small can often work better. Remember, you are guaranteed to write a unique essay if you focus on something you have experienced or found meaning in through experience.

For instance, writing an essay on what it felt like to drive a car alone for the first time or why you enjoy preparing a favorite recipe can showcase your creativity and ability to make connections with something larger than yourself.

When Alex tackled the "ethical dilemma" prompt, he chose a minor but telling incident from his family vacation trip: when he returned a wallet he had found. His 400-word essay traced his panic, cultural pressure, and ultimate choice to do the right thing. That simple moment gave admissions a window into his integrity far more powerfully than any grand project could have.

Currently, the Common Application offers seven prompts to choose from. You will be asked to select one prompt and write an essay answering it in 650 words or fewer. Here they are, along with percentage of students who choose each:

1. Background, Identity, Interest, or Talent (18%)

Some students have a background, identity, interest, or talent that is so meaningful they believe their application would be incomplete without it. If this sounds like you, then please share your story.

2. Obstacle or Challenge (22%) The lessons we take from obstacles we encounter can be fundamental to later success. Recount a time when you faced a challenge, setback, or failure. How did it affect you, and what did you learn?

3. Belief or Idea Challenged (3%) Reflect on a time when you questioned or challenged a belief or idea. What prompted your thinking? What was the outcome?

4. Gratitude or Acts of Kindness (3%) Reflect on something that someone has done for you that has made you happy or thankful in a surprising way. How has this gratitude affected or motivated you?

5. Personal Growth or Accomplishment (20%) Discuss an accomplishment, event, or realization that sparked a period of personal growth and a new understanding of yourself or others.

6. Passion or Topic that Captivates You (5%) Describe a topic, idea, or concept you find so engaging it makes you lose all track of time. Why does it captivate you? What or who do you turn to when you want to learn more?

7. Topic of Your Choice (28%) Share an essay on any topic of your choice. It can be one you've already written, one that responds to a different prompt, or one of your own design.

Planning the writing process should be divided into three parts:

Part 1: Choose your prompt and draft your Common Application essay (the 650-word personal statement) as a separate project in its own document. Using the Common Application topics as a guide can be helpful if you often struggle with deciding what to write about. The Common App prompt is just a starting point; it gives your essay a frame, but it shouldn't dictate your story. Don't make the mistake of choosing a prompt first and then trying to force a story into it. What matters more is the story you need to tell. Start by brainstorming the experiences, turning points, and moments that reveal something real about who you are. Once you've clarified that, the right prompt will naturally align.

Create several outlines, then focus on writing about a topic or idea that has had a profound personal impact on you. Remember, the word "personal" is very important; discussing topics that interest you, such as "Why I want world peace" or "How I plan to eradicate homelessness," could distract you from your main goal of revealing something about yourself. Some research indicates that, in recent years, students have often chosen topics such as challenging a specific idea or concept as their favorites. This may be because such topics combine factual knowledge with a personal perspective, offering students a good starting point to write about a real issue. However, there is a downside: Balancing expertise with a strong personal focus can be challenging.

Part 2: Draft all your supplemental essays in one working document, titled Supplemental Essays. Why? Because many colleges ask similar questions about your identity, interests, values, academic goals, or reasons for choosing a particular major. By grouping your responses together in one place, you can identify patterns, cut down on repetition, and reuse strong material across different applications without starting from scratch each time. Supplemental essays also require you to research each school thoroughly, including academic majors, curriculum, graduation outcomes, community, clubs, and other extracurricular activities that are important to you.

Part 3: Assemble your portfolio and any extra materials such as writing samples, projects, videos, and artwork. This will be specific to your major if you're applying to programs like screenwriting, graphic design, art, architecture, or engineering. Many preprofessional majors also require additional items like essays, detailed research portfolios, and videos before you can be invited for an interview.

FROM SCATTERED TO STRATEGIC: ORGANIZING YOUR WAY IN

KEY TAKEAWAYS:

- Every part of the Common App (and supplements) helps frame who you are.

- Focus first on crafting your story, not just answering their questions.

- The topic you pick matters less than what it reveals about you.

- Early organization saves you from chaos later, so prioritize research, planning, and story mapping.

CHAPTER 8

Can't Pick a Prompt? You're Not Alone; Here's What to Do

> IT'S NOT ABOUT PICKING THE PERFECT PROMPT. IT'S ABOUT FINDING THE STORY ONLY YOU CAN TELL.

Many students spend weeks trying to guess which topic is the least popular among candidates, so they can write about it, hoping to stand out from the crowd. This is useless guesswork. Take this Common Application topic, for example: *Reflect on something that someone has done for you that has made you happy or thankful in a surprising way*. At first glance, this topic is a straightforward way to write a unique essay.

The same trap appears in this Common Application prompt: *Describe a character in fiction, a historical figure, or a creative work that has had an influence on you, and describe that influence.* Again, it looks promising. Both prompts dangle an emotional hook–gratitude, admiration, inspiration–but they funnel students toward essays that sound generic. What feels profound to you often reads like déjà vu to an admissions reader.

But you'd be surprised to know that your chosen hero's name is favored by many others. It's challenging to choose a famous person who hasn't already been the subject of thousands of admissions essays. Second on the list of the overdone person of influence essays are relatives (parents and grandparents are the overwhelming favorites), followed closely by coaches. If you do choose the "gratitude" topic, but stick to a generic answer, be fully aware of the cliché potential. Your focus here is on getting creative in how you explain the person's influence on you, or what is that special thing someone did to make you thankful. A parent's guidance or a coach's leadership is meaningful, yes, but what makes this essay about you? How unique are your parents' guidance or your coach's leadership abilities? No matter who you write about, remember that the question is a catalyst for revealing information about you, not about your person of influence.

I have seen students write about their teachers, grandparents, parents, and uncles. Having a role model of influence is great, but only if you relate their impact to your own life. In the end, every strong response answers two questions clearly: *How* and *why* it matters to you. It's always about you and your experience.

Instead of focusing on the apparent heroism or wisdom, highlight the *unexpected* way that person shaped you.

- Example: Instead of "Watching my grandmother make pancakes for me even when sick taught me care and perseverance," write about how her obsession with coupon-clipping made you a data-driven economist.

CAN'T PICK A PROMPT? YOU'RE NOT ALONE; HERE'S WHAT TO DO

This reframes a common figure into a fresh, quirky influence that says more about *you* than about her. This kind of prompt will work only if you shift the spotlight back to you.

Make the admired figure the backdrop, not the star. Focus on your reaction, your evolution, your decisions.

- Example: Instead of writing "Einstein inspires me because he was brilliant," you could say: "I once taped a photo of Einstein sticking out his tongue to my desk, and every time I bombed a math problem, it reminded me that genius looks silly too. That gave me the courage to keep going."

- Why it works: The person is just a catalyst—the essay's real subject is how you deal with setbacks and grow from them.

Admissions officers will appreciate essays that show **fallibility, imperfection, or ordinariness** in someone typically idolized because it makes the writer look more self-aware and original.

Michael Jordan: Overused as "the greatest," but less cliché if you focus on him being cut from his high school team and how *that* became the source of his drive. You connect it to your own rejections.

J.K. Rowling: Instead of saying "she inspires me as an author," write about the twelve publishers who turned her down. You connect it to your own college rejections and the persistence to keep creating.

Your math teacher: Not because they "inspired you," but because they once admitted they flunked geometry in high school and had to retake it. That honesty freed you to fail without shame.

Your parent: Not because they "taught you resilience," but because you once watched them burn dinner three nights in a row before finally getting it right. That became your lesson in trial-and-error.

Frida Kahlo: Not just "she was a bold artist," but "she painted flat on her back in bed after surgeries." You tie it to working through your own limitations.

Take the "flawed" side of a giant and turn it around to show the personal and ordinary side and connect it to your own.

Here is a college-specific example: *Describe a character in fiction, a historical figure, or a creative work (as in art, music, science, etc.) that has influenced you, and explain that influence.* This is a very similar prompt to the one above, but it has now expanded the options to include a fictional character or a historical figure. As with this choice, keep the focus on yourself, not the character or creative work. The hidden agenda here is that once you disclose your character or figure of influence, we will know what influences you, what motivates you to do the things you do, who you are, and what matters to you. If you want to find out everything about someone without asking them direct questions, ask about their favorite movie, book, or character. Answering this prompt is not easy to do, especially if you choose an obscure character or work that can't be explained in a short paragraph. Your choice of topic does disclose something about you, but you need to reveal even more by showing how these characters have influenced you. Remember to stay on task.

The best way to approach this topic is to choose someone or something that the reader has probably heard of; too much description or background information is a waste of words that should be used to write about yourself.

Another twist might come from a prompt that inquires about your academic career. Here is another college-specific version: *Given your background, describe an experience that illustrates what you would bring to the diversity of a college community or an encounter that has demonstrated the importance of diversity to you.* Diversity is a key word in admissions today. While admissions offices have always sought to create classes with a wide range of abilities, viewpoints, and backgrounds (imagine if every first-year student were a leader, a gymnast, or a drummer), in recent years, schools are even more eager to tout the diversity of their student body. Again, the focus is on you, not your parents, not your family's journey. Therefore, aim to spend at least eighty percent of the essay demonstrating what you bring to the table. Use a specific anecdote to illustrate your growth, values, or perspective; plan to show, rather than tell.

KEY TAKEAWAYS:

- Diversity prompts aren't just about background; they're about the mindset and growth you bring.

- Picking the right prompt isn't about avoiding clichés; it's about owning your real experience with depth and clarity.

- The essay reflects who you are, not just what you think Admissions wants to hear.

CHAPTER 9

How to Start: It's All About You (in 650 Words)

> UNCOVERING YOUR IDENTITY IS A LIFELONG PURSUIT.

Let's face it: Six hundred and fifty words might sound like a lot, but when you're trying to cram your entire existence, dreams, quirks, and deepest secrets into it, it suddenly feels like squeezing an elephant into a suitcase. Spoiler alert: You'll need to start writing early to maximize your chance of turning the big pressure into a big opportunity.

Every year, I see students who think they're writing a statement of purpose instead of a personal statement. They missed the memo about the magic of the word "personal." Don't be that person. This essay isn't about sounding like an academic robot; it's about you. The real you. The one who has a thing for obscure '80s music, builds weird stuff (don't mention LEGOs, please), or secretly dreams of becoming a dog whisperer.

I had a student write about his obsession with wearing mismatched socks to feel less self-conscious. It began as a mistake on a busy morning. He received so many comments and struck up conversations about it that he made it a point to do it regularly to force himself into the spotlight, and as a result, improve his people skills. He turned that into his personal statement anchor, as undoubtedly the incident had given him a lot to think about and work on regarding himself.

But if the idea of writing an essay makes you want to crawl under the covers, hear me out. Start small.

Here's the deal: Writing clearly, objectively, and persuasively takes time and practice. Think of it as training for a marathon, except instead of running, you're working those brain muscles. And if writing isn't your strong suit, don't panic. It's not like the admissions officers are expecting the next Shakespeare. They just want to know you.

"But wait," you're saying, "I've got SATs, ACTs, APs, clubs, debates, and Netflix episodes piling up. How am I supposed to fit in essay writing?" Breathe. Start with baby steps. Scribble down random ideas, funny moments, big lessons, the time your team lost that game and blamed it on you, or when you could barely hold back your tears from a breakup. This book is here to guide you from messy drafts to polished brilliance.

Now let's talk about what not to do. Are you tempted to write about how your debate team totally should have won nationals or how you single-handedly fixed your robotics team's coding disaster at 3 a.m.? Don't. These stories are great for family dinners, but not for your college essay. Admissions officers want to know about you, not your team. As a rule, I tell my students to spot all the "we" pronouns in the essay and rephrase those sentences.

And while we're at it, please don't sprinkle your essay with quotes from Mother Teresa, Martin Luther King, or random philosophers you found on Pinterest. It's your essay, not theirs. The same goes for writing about how your grandma's struggle inspired your career choice. Grandma and Grandpa sound amazing, but let's keep the focus on why you should be the one heading to college, not them.

The bottom line? This essay is your chance to be unapologetically your glorious self. There is no need to sound like a TED Talk speaker or an eighteenth-century philosopher. Just tell a story that only you can tell. Be honest, be real, and maybe even make them laugh a little, but only if humor is your forte.

Perfect practice makes perfect, and this is your chance to show the world who you are. So, grab that pen (or keyboard) and get started.

As I mentioned earlier, a great place to start is by thinking of your stories and making a list. Brainstorming doesn't have to mean staring at a blank page until your brain implodes. Instead, it can be a matter of jotting down small, seemingly unrelated moments. The second approach is to consider each prompt closely. Reading the question thoroughly is more than a checkbox; it's an essential strategy.

What kind of prompt are you responding to? Is it asking you a question—like *why* or *how*—or giving you a command, such as *describe*? I can't stress enough the importance of starting early to give yourself the chance to analyze the prompts and gather your ideas. There's always a friend who will tell you they wrote their essays at the last minute, and that's how they got into a Top Ten. Don't let someone else's exception become your rule. Starting early gives you the advantage of time to reflect and make revisions for work that truly stands out.

Write out the full title/prompt; don't be tempted to shorten it, as this can be misleading. Ensure you are aware of the word limit and begin to highlight or underline key words in the prompt. Display the title on your working document so you can always see it. It serves as a reminder and helps you stay focused on the question.

At this point, a question might come to mind: Am I ready? No one explains it better than writer Jason Arnopp: "... Sometimes you're not ready to write a script because you *haven't finished thinking about it*." This is the clearest statement about "writing readiness."

Often, you've spent days or months doing the brainwork, thinking about it. Maybe you even saw the first paragraph of your story in a dream. So, should you go for it, like pressing the big red button just to see what happens, and make a big mess? Sometimes you're just not ready. But the truth is, you might never know unless you make that mess, and that's completely okay. Many students wait to start writing, thinking they need to wait until they become better writers and gain more life experience.

For you, like most students, the most challenging part might be getting started. You might have a story in your mind but feel unsure how to begin, or you may not know where to start. Both situations are common. Don't hold yourself back; experiment and try different writing outlines, because it's hard to know what works until you try. Creating an outline and plotting the initial story might seem tedious, but planning the first parts can help. It's all about the first draft. Remember this: Your first draft isn't a masterpiece; it's not supposed to be. Only you will see it, so don't put too much pressure on yourself.

KEY TAKEAWAYS:

- Always have a plan on when and how to start, even a loose one.

- The exact plan doesn't matter as much as the act of thinking about it every day and adjusting when needed.

- Study the prompts and brainstorm ideas in preparation for your first draft.

- Daily check-ins with your plan keep you honest, consistent, and moving forward, even if your progress is small.

CHAPTER 10

Breaking Down a Prompt Word by Word and Reading Between the Lines

> A GOOD ESSAY DOESN'T START WHEN YOU BEGIN WRITING; IT STARTS THE MOMENT YOU READ THE PROMPT WITH CURIOSITY.

One of the most popular prompts among students in recent years asks:

Reflect on a time when you questioned or challenged a belief or idea. What prompted your thinking? What was the outcome?

If this prompt makes your brain freeze, don't worry. The trick is to break it down word by word, phrase by phrase, so the daunting task becomes manageable.

Let's start with the first word: **reflect**. It's a verb that means to look back in time, to revisit a "once upon a time" moment in your life. This indicates that your essay requires a clear story arc: a beginning (what happened), a middle (the challenge), and an end (what you learned). Think of it as a "zero to hero" story where you gain new insights or a fresh perspective.

Now, let's look at the verbs: **questioned** and **challenged**.

Questioning evokes curiosity. It might involve other people or events you either observed or directly experienced. It suggests exploring something unfamiliar, like asking why your family's traditions work a certain way or pondering societal norms.

Challenged, on the other hand, feels like action. There's resistance, even confrontation. When you say the word "challenged," doesn't it feel bolder than "questioned"? This is about taking a stand, perhaps even against someone else's expectations or ideas.

Ask yourself: Does your story lean toward curiosity or resistance? Which word best captures your experience? Next, let's move to **belief** versus **idea**.

A **belief** is deeply rooted. It's part of your identity, shaped by your upbringing, culture, or values. It's something you would defend because it defines who you are.

An **idea**, by contrast, is more fleeting. It's like a spark of inspiration or a hypothesis you play with but haven't fully committed to yet.

Do you notice the difference? The prompt asks you to choose a lane: Are you questioning a fleeting idea or challenging a belief that anchors your worldview?

Understanding the nuances of the prompt helps you focus. It encourages you to dig deeper and consider which part of your story to tell and how to frame it. For instance, you once challenged your school's dress code. Was that about questioning the practicality of the rules (idea)? Or was it a deeper challenge to societal norms regarding self-expression (belief)?

By dissecting the prompt this way, you ensure that your essay directly answers the question. This isn't just about telling a good story; it's about demonstrating how you think, reflect, and grow.

When you combine the strength of the words from the question in this way, you realize that the story will need to follow a different tempo and rhythm based on the words. Are you narrating a story or reflecting on an event? Choose your style.

THE PLOT TWIST IS YOU

KEY TAKEAWAYS:

- Breaking down the questions will help you sort out the key words that hold the key to a successful essay.

- Choose which way you want your story to go.

CHAPTER 11

Prewriting and Brainstorming Like a Pro

> A GREAT STORY ISN'T ABOUT WHAT HAPPENED. IT'S ABOUT WHO CHANGED AND HOW.

Often, I remind students of the subtle differences between brainstorming and prewriting. How do these two differ? Once you have some ideas or just a few words that describe you as a person, you have completed the brainstorming process. You can brainstorm ten different meanings for the same word until you find the one that best expresses your vision. Prewriting comes next. It is a powerful way to begin without the stress of crafting a final, tangible essay. How does that work? Prewriting, as the name suggests, puts you at ease because it implies that all you are doing is warming up. Knowing this should relax your mind, silencing the critic's voice and freeing you to develop strong ideas. Think of your first draft like a rough TikTok edit: It's not polished, but it's the start of something great.

One commonality among students' first drafts is the description of early childhood experiences. This can be very helpful to start with, as it is usually the easiest way to get ideas flowing. For the college essay, you will primarily focus on your teenage years, high school life, and personal growth. However, starting with kindergarten and following a chronological line of events will provide the most detailed narrative and is often the simplest way to begin your story. Consider yourself the main character in this narrative and keep the storyline straight by highlighting key events, challenges, triumphs, and turning points.

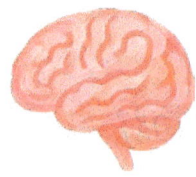

Here are some questions designed to help you discover your unique stories.

The purpose of this exercise is to help you see your life as a coherent story, identifying patterns, significant moments, and themes that have shaped who you are.

1. Can You Name Your Values and Beliefs?

Exercise: This step can be done even before you begin writing, during the stage of creating your college list. It involves listing your core values and beliefs. Doing this early can help you identify the driving forces behind your choices and understand why you are making them. Why are you seeking a college, an activity, or a major, and what inner values and beliefs drive that choice? For each one, describe a specific experience that reinforced or challenged this value or belief.

Purpose: Understanding your values and beliefs can help you identify what truly matters to you and why, providing a foundation for your personal narrative.

2. Can You Identify Meaningful Memories?

Exercise: Identify three of your most meaningful memories. Describe each memory in detail, emphasizing its significance and how it impacted you.

Purpose: This helps you pinpoint moments that have profoundly impacted your personal development and that can be pivotal points in your essay.

3. How Have You Overcome Adversity?

Exercise: Reflect on a time when you faced a significant challenge or adversity. Describe the situation, how you responded, what you learned, and how it changed you.

Purpose: Highlighting how you have overcome challenges showcases resilience and personal growth, which are key attributes that colleges seek in applicants.

4. Who Are Your Heroes and Role Models?

Exercise: Reflect on the people you admire and identify your heroes. Describe who they are, why you admire them, and how they have influenced your life and sense of purpose.

This will help you understand the qualities you value in others and how they align with your goals and identity.

5. What Is Your Ideal Future Self?

Exercise: Picture yourself ten years from now. Describe who you are, what you're doing, and what you've accomplished. Reflect on how your current choices are shaping your future.

Purpose: This exercise prompts you to reflect on your long-term goals and the steps necessary to achieve them, aligning your present actions with your future aspirations.

6. Can You Make a List of Your Values?

Exercise: Create a thorough list of personal values (e.g., honesty, kindness, ambition, curiosity, sensitivity). Organize them in ascending order of significance and provide a brief explanation for your top five values, including specific examples from your life that illustrate each one.

Purpose: To help clarify your motivations and principles that guide your actions and decisions.

7. Can You Share Your Daily Reflections?

Exercise: For one week, maintain a daily journal in which you reflect on your experiences, thoughts, and feelings. At the end of the week, review your entries and identify any recurring themes or insights that arise.

Purpose: Regular reflection increases your awareness of thoughts and feelings, uncovering essential patterns and themes for your essay.

8. Can You Identify Important Defining Moments?

Exercise: Identify and write about three defining moments in your life. Describe each moment in detail, focusing on how it influenced your identity and life direction. These moments can be moving to a new country, changing schools, a health crisis, losing a family member, welcoming a new family member, getting a pet, or meeting a new friend.

Purpose: Defining moments are pivotal in shaping who you are and can provide powerful narratives for your college essay.

How can you implement these exercises?

1. Set aside time. Dedicate specific times to create a quiet, reflective environment for these exercises. Listen to your favorite music and eliminate noise and friends' chatter so you can focus on yourself. I have a student who came to our meeting one day and declared with visible satisfaction that he had finally come up with the introduction part of his essay—in the shower. He shared that in his crowded household, this was one place where he could "hear himself think."

2. Review and reflect. After completing the exercises, review your responses to identify common themes and standout stories.

3. Discuss with others. Share reflections with trusted friends, family, or mentors to gain additional perspectives and insights. Do they recognize you in these descriptions? How true and real are you in your self-assessment?

If you are the kind of writer who thinks in layers, or if you find yourself wanting to say more than the structure allows, the late writer David Foster Wallace has a technique for you. Wallace is known for his footnotes and dense reflections. He found ways to delve deeply while keeping readers engaged. You can adapt this style to suit your own needs. In a college essay, a similar strategy could help you introduce an aside or insight that doesn't quite fit into the main flow but still adds value. Study how Wallace often utilized footnotes and digressions to enhance depth, humor, and additional context in his writing. This technique can make your essay more engaging and nuanced.

Here are some examples of how Wallace's techniques can work for you:

Footnotes. In your essay, you could write, "Winning the science fair was the pinnacle of my middle school career," and add a footnote reading, "This might sound hyperbolic; however, considering the competition and my previous year's catastrophic attempt at a volcano model that failed to erupt, it felt like a monumental achievement."

Implementation: Use footnotes sparingly to add humorous asides or extra context without disrupting the main narrative flow.

Intricate and playful language. One of the most memorable elements of Wallace's prose is its rich vocabulary and playful use of language. This should not discourage or intimidate you; just do your best. At this stage of the process, you cannot go wrong. Utilize a varied and precise vocabulary to make your essay stand out. Instead of writing, "I felt nervous during the debate," try: "My nerves resembled a jittery orchestra tuning up before a high-stakes symphony performance, each note a reminder of the impending crescendo."

Implementation: Experiment with metaphors and similes to craft vivid, memorable descriptions. However, ensure that your language stays clear and does not obscure your meaning.

Personal reflection and depth. Wallace's essays often dive deeply into personal reflection, examining his thoughts and emotions with honesty and complexity.

Example: "Upon reflection, my initial disdain for group projects stemmed less from the projects themselves and more from my fear of relinquishing control and trusting others with my grade and, by extension, my future."

Implementation: Dig deeply into your feelings and experiences. Reflect not only on what happened but also on what mattered and how it shaped you. Authenticity is essential.

Blending humor with seriousness. Wallace had a knack for mixing humor with serious topics, making his writing entertaining and profound. Example: "Failing my first driving test was, at the time, a catastrophe of epic proportions, comparable only to the great Spilled Milk Incident of my toddler years."

Implementation: You can balance your essay by weaving in lighthearted anecdotes or humorous observations that complement the more serious aspects of your story.

Here's a short essay that incorporates these techniques. The first three paragraphs are the main narrative, and the fourth is where humor/seriousness comes in:

Applying to college felt like navigating an intricate labyrinth, each turn laden with anticipatory hope or impending doom. The day I received my acceptance letter from Stanford remains etched in my memory. As I tore open the envelope, my heart pounded with the ferocity of a timpani drum in a Wagnerian opera.

For context, this was after several weeks of compulsively refreshing my email inbox, a ritual that had become so ingrained it was practically a muscle memory.

The relief that washed over me was not only about securing a spot at my dream school; it represented the culmination of years spent grappling with self-doubt and the nagging fear that my best efforts might never be enough. Reflecting on this journey, I realize that each setback, like when my meticulously constructed science project succumbed to an ill-timed sprinkler malfunction, taught me resilience and the value of adaptability.

Of course, this resilience was also tested by more mundane adversities, such as my ill-fated attempt at culinary independence during freshman year, resulting in a kitchen fire and an impromptu lesson in fire safety.

By drawing on David Foster Wallace's unique techniques of added depth, you can effortlessly use playful language and achieve deep personal reflection (maybe even some humor). This is an easy way to add more insightful messages stealthily. You can create a college application essay that is both engaging and reflective of your voice.

CHAPTER 12

Find Your Focus and Sharpen Your Story: The Formula for a Standout Essay

> AUTHENTICITY ISN'T ABOUT SAYING EVERYTHING. IT'S ABOUT DESCRIBING THE RIGHT MOMENTS EFFECTIVELY.

My students ask me: Is there a magic formula for writing a compelling college essay? Not exactly. However, there *is* a formula, and while it might feel more like math than magic, it's effective. Let me walk you through it:

(Character + Situation) x Obstacles = New You (where character = you)

Use the formula well, and you'll create a story that feels like magic. You, the character, enter a situation, face obstacles, and emerge changed. That transformation is the heart of your essay, whether the ending is triumphant, bittersweet, or quietly reflective.

And even if you don't find the formula helpful, it is guaranteed to assist with this one ingredient, which is probably the most important part of the process so far: the focal point in your story. A focused essay doesn't just tell a story; it forges a connection. By highlighting a single point or idea, you'll leave the reader with a clear picture of who you are and what matters most to you.

Think of your essay like a photograph: What's in the focus square? Is it crisp, or crowded with distractions? Every focus square has a purpose. Find it. In one focus square, you might show your ambition. In another, your frustration. In another, the overwhelming difficulty of what you're facing. If a scene inside the focus square doesn't have a purpose, your reader will feel it — and not in a good way.

When writing, keep this word in mind: **focus**. Without it, your essay becomes a blur of too many details, too little clarity. Strong essays focus on one subject and let the rest fade into the background. Don't cram in every high school highlight. That's what your activities list is for. Your essay should reveal who you are through *one defining idea*. Here's how to find the focus of your story:

Hospital volunteering? Don't summarize the role. Tell us about one patient interaction that changed how you see empathy or responsibility.

Running cross-country? Don't rehash victories. Take us on a long run. What did you think about? What drove you forward?

Photography award? Skip the trophy. Talk about what you see differently through the lens and why it matters.

With only about 650 words to tell your story, a lack of focus can turn your essay into a laundry list instead of a compelling snapshot of who you are. Additionally, a confusing narrative can even weaken the strengths of your application. One of the biggest issues with many essays, even the best ones out there, is how little logical sense they actually make. They hook you early, draw you in, and then about a minute later, the reader realizes that you, the main character, are in some strange game of literary Twister. Who is who? What is what? Suddenly, plot holes become so big you could lose a truckload of Stanley Cups in them.

Don't underestimate the readers' comprehension and attention span. They'll notice if you bring clean water to children in an Indian village on Monday and then, without explanation, win first place in the Intel Science Competition on Tuesday with no background to support it. So, unless you have teleportation tech hidden in your backpack, no one is crossing 2,000 miles of ocean in a single day.

Even though it might be difficult to do, as you write your college essay, ask yourself: *Does this make sense?* If the admissions officer is likely to mutter, "Really?" then you've lost them.

When you're writing about yourself, remember that, like every main character in a story, you have needs, wants, and fears. You've been reading stories since you were a little child, and you know how they go: John wants a boat. Sally fears failing her driver's test. Nova the Star Panda needs to collect stardust sprinkles, or the galaxy ice cream will melt. Whatever the details, every character in a story is driven by something. That drive is the force that moves them forward. When you're writing, clearly show what motivates you; motivations are the fuel that drives the plot.

Colleges need geniuses to maintain a steady academic pace and eccentricity to counterbalance the all-work, no-play mentality. They need artists and musicians to bring beauty and leaders to provide vision and direction. They also need athletes who will gather everyone for a fun game and foster a spirited college atmosphere. There is a place for all of you: math whizzes and quiz bowl champions, travel enthusiasts, future philanthropists, and dreamers.

But here is the question: Which version of yourself are you showing them?

You've heard it a dozen times: "Just be yourself." It sounds comforting. But which version of "yourself" are you showing? Your school self? Your gamer or artist self? The self from the robotics club?

A better goal: Be your *best* self. The one aligned with your values and your aspirations.

Being authentic doesn't mean being unfiltered. This isn't a diary; it's a crafted narrative. The best essays reflect who you are becoming, not just who you've been. Raw honesty without purpose isn't vulnerability, but a missed opportunity. Choosing a story that reflects your character, growth, and voice is important, but so is polishing it with thought and intention. Don't confuse "being real" with turning in a rough draft. Admissions officers want to see clarity, structure, and depth, not a stream-of-consciousness monologue.

Admissions will judge you based on the current set of data you submit, such as grades and standardized scores, but only to use it as a prediction of your potential. Similarly, the best college essays aren't about who you are. They're about who you're becoming. If you cling too tightly to the "this is just me" narrative, you may miss the opportunity to showcase your growth, ambition, and capacity for evolution.

Expect to write many drafts. Start with a long one, at a thousand words or more, and then refine it. Cut what's verbose or off topic and keep only the most essential details for context. Only after the core message is tight should you look for "icing on the cake" analogies, metaphors, and cultural references that enhance your point, but keep it real because not every day will feel like a parade. Some days the words flow; other days it's like trying to rescue a single AirPod from the abyss of your backpack. But overall, you should find some enjoyment in what you're creating. If you're miserable while writing, there's a good chance your reader will feel that, too.

But whichever direction your story takes, never push a narrative at the expense of clarity. Always return to this: *What's the one thing I want the reader to remember?* As a writer, you are the puppet master. You're pulling strings to make the audience feel something: inspiration, triumph, hope, nostalgia, even laughter. Don't leave it to chance, but instead decide what you want them to feel in each scene and guide them there.

CHAPTER 13

Learning Storytelling from Disney

> "IF YOU CAN DREAM IT, YOU CAN DO IT."
> — WALT DISNEY

The quote above says it all! Let's be honest, if there is a place on earth that knows how to tell stories for a living and how to make people live in a dream, that is Disney. And as much as I would like to say that what Disney did is take a good story and commercialize it, the fact remains: The Walt Disney Studios and its writers, producers, and directors are the best at telling stories in a way that sticks. So, what are they doing right that we can learn and emulate?

1. Disney states the status quo. Disney movies begin by describing the current situation and some basic rules about what is and isn't allowed. This sets up the need for adventure. The Little Mermaid is captivated by the human world just by watching sailors and their belongings enter the ocean. She feels she belongs to a different world, and her growing longing leads her to a witch who happily makes a devilish deal with the innocent mermaid.

What you should do: To start your story, begin to think of a set of rules that contradict your dreams and ambitions. Describe the status quo and outline a plan for getting out of it.

Your turn: _____
_____
_____
_____
_____
_____

2. Disney names the challenges. Every protagonist in a film faces challenges greater than themselves. These challenges vary but are always numerous and more difficult than anything the hero has encountered before. Belle encounters the Beast to save her father. Ariel must navigate the cruelty of the human world. Moana must overcome self-doubt and external enemies from all directions on land and sea. Mulan faces an army of enemies and stands alone among her people because of gender stereotypes. Yet, all of them overcome these challenges and temptations to give up, only to see things worsen before they get better.

What you should do: Define your goals and be ready to fight for what you believe, as it will not come easily.

Your turn: _____
_____
_____
_____
_____
_____
_____

3. Disney often drops the hero into a moment of deep despair, then delivers a powerful revelation that reignites hope. It's the emotional low point that makes the comeback feel even bigger: Just when events look like they are about to reach their peak after the protagonist has overcome all hurdles, a sudden twist eventually comes. Rapunzel is on cloud nine and has achieved all that she would have wanted and more, until the inevitable comes: Mother Gothel cleverly recaptures her prize, and Rapunzel becomes subject to despair when she realizes that her dream was not what it had seemed. Moana has lost her companion following a defeat, and she is ready to give up; however, she then has a dramatic return after recalling her heritage and diving into the ocean to continue her expedition alone. Appealing to emotion sparks a reaction in your audience.

What you should do: Following despair comes the realization of hope, like a ray of sun bursting through a torrential storm. Describe your "aha" moment of realization and invite the audience to feel the relief and the excitement. This is where you describe your new normal and your vision of the future.

Your turn: _____
_____
_____
_____
_____
_____
_____

And while Disney's stories stop at "lived happily ever after," yours shouldn't. Go on and make a sequel! Continue to push the limits of your imagination and continue to create a gripping and exciting adventure. One core understanding that you should adhere to that will guide you to writing a memorable personal statement is this: Be the character who is trying for more than just their own successes.

KEY TAKEAWAYS:

- Describe your current status quo and give enough context.

- Decide the emotion you want the reader to feel; every sentence should work toward that feeling.

CHAPTER 14

Where the Rubber Meets the Road: Examples of Successful Personal Statements

> GOOD WRITING IS ABOUT FLAIR AND FRICTION WITH ENOUGH TENSION TO LEAVE A MARK.

Let's examine some students' work and see how each has identified a central focus.

Essay Focus: Overcoming a Challenge
- Private high school
- 4.2 GPA
- Accepted to a Top Ten
- Pre-med major

Reflect on a time when you questioned or challenged a belief or idea. What prompted your thinking? What was the outcome?

Mod Pizza is a relatively unimportant fast-food joint for the average person. However, in my eyes, at the ripe old age of fifteen, its welcoming aroma turned me into Augustus Gloop in Willy Wonka's Chocolate Factory. Going down the line, I stacked pepperoni toppings till I'd achieved the meat-lovers' delight.

With the box in hand, I didn't waste a second to bite into the meaty goodness. The burst of spices tickled my taste buds and exceeded what I had imagined for years; from that moment on, my life as a vegetarian was over, and a whole new world of flavors had opened to me. My vegetarian Eastern Orthodox mom and Hindu vegan dad (unless cake is involved) looked away as I entertained my tongue with this new delicacy. To them, meat was unnecessary and harmful to the soul, and I'd been raised to believe so.

As someone who loved all animals, showing them compassion wasn't hard. Many pets came and went in our household as my parents and I struggled to feed them live critters. Each case strengthened my belief in vegetarianism. As my faith in their teachings grew, so did the extent to which my imagination exaggerated the consequences. Much like the moral decay hidden within Dorian Gray's portrait, images of corrupted and withering souls within people's bodies filled my mind.

However, as a competitive athlete with fewer hours of rest, I began feeling the effects of my diet. When I decided to pursue Épée fencing, I was drawn to the elegance and strategy of the sport. It's logical that chivalry fulfilled my childhood fantasy of being a modern-age King Arthur, but that demanded rigorous training and physical and mental stamina. Crashing in bed after a long day with cramping muscles and stomach pangs, I craved more than a meal of rice and lentils. Such morsels left me feeling like Tantalus, eternally tormented by unattainable desires, tantalized by the dangling fruit out of reach. An imaginary, glowing turkey hung before me, tempting me, but years of listening to my parents (alluding to Manu-Samhita scriptures about slaughter and sin) kept me from grabbing it. An impromptu conversation with my coach about my diet confirmed my fears: I needed a regimented, non-vegetarian diet to improve my athletic performance.

This was my turning point, as I faced a choice that went beyond mere food and dietary preferences; it was about upholding tradition and preserving my identity. Fencing has always been, and continues to be, the source of my self-expression, creativity, and pride, and I refuse to let anything hinder my performance. It became clear that there was no singular correct approach to dietary choices.

The problem I began to face was that cultural identity, such as food, had become a central part of my family relations. It felt as if changing my relationship with food was a barrier to cultural transmission and a part of my identity, deriving from this heritage. In a world driven by categorizations and labels, it became essential to pause and reflect on the limitations they imposed on my life. While the stories I'd heard provided a sense of identity and belonging, they oversimplified complex realities. They hindered my understanding of my individuality, ideas, and ideals of who I wanted to be and where I was going.

Unbeknownst to me, these experiences challenged me to think criti-

cally about traditions and preconceived notions, even if someone argues about the science behind them. My passion for fencing and my love for family are like a well-strategized game that requires adaptation. I have improved as both an athlete and a person because I have found a harmonious balance between my heritage and my evolving identity. I may have started this adventure as Augustus Gloop eyeing those chocolate rivers at Willy Wonka's factory, but now, I've authored a new story with my understanding of the world and my role in it.

The challenge I faced was cultural identity, especially since food had become a key part of my family bonds. Changing how I related to food felt like it blocked cultural transmission and was a part of my identity tied to my heritage. In a world focused on labels and categories, it was important to pause and consider how they limited me. While the stories I heard gave me a sense of identity and belonging, they also simplified complex realities. They hindered my understanding of people, as well as my own thoughts and goals about who I wanted to be and where I was headed.

Why It Worked

Although the prompts are the same for all students using the Common Application, each student possesses a unique style. You might not yet consider yourself a writer with a distinct voice. When you finish writing your essay, you'll have a better understanding of yourself both as a person and as a writer. But until then, how do you determine your writing style? One stylistic option is to adopt the "change of status quo" style, also known as the problem-solving essay, as illustrated here. This style emphasizes transformation and growth, often centered around a specific challenge or obstacle you've encountered. It's a narrative-driven approach with a clear structure. Think of it as a story arc where you, the protagonist, start in a challenging or imperfect situation, face obstacles, and ultimately emerge stronger, wiser, or more capable.

How can this style work well for you? This type of personal statement illustrates how you confront and overcome adversity, providing concrete evidence of resilience and adaptability. It's inspiring and relatable, often leaving readers (the admissions representative) rooting for you. It will be effective if you employ key writing techniques, such as vivid sensory details, that allow the reader to "see" your surroundings and to feel your feelings. Use descriptive elements that create the immersive feeling of being there. Highlighting moments of struggle will build tension and make the resolution satisfying. The essay should conclude with you reflecting on how the experience shaped you, considering not just what happened, but why it mattered to you as a person and to your future.

For example, you might write about persevering through a demanding academic project, navigating family responsibilities, or finding your voice in a competitive extracurricular activity. The core elements of this kind of writing will be a clear challenge or conflict (external or internal), a turning point or moment of realization, a resolution, personal growth, or accomplishment. The core here is a central idea or theme that connects disparate experiences. The focus is on your actions and the outcomes that demonstrate personal growth.

The following essay is a reflective narrative written in response to the last (and least chosen by students) prompt, "Share an essay on any topic of your choice." It demonstrates a reflective style that is more complex to execute because it lacks a specific conclusion or measurable progress. It takes a quieter but equally powerful approach by exploring your inner world, delving into your thoughts, values, and the ideas that define you. It's less about what happened to you and more about how you see the world and interpret your experiences.

The focus is inward, on introspection and self-discovery, and the writing is studded with literary techniques such as metaphor, imagery, and symbolism.

This essay showcases your depth of thought and ability to articulate complex emotions or abstract ideas. It's particularly effective if you find meaning in the subtleties of everyday life or wish to highlight your creativity and intellectual curiosity. To achieve this successfully, you should review key writing techniques, such as literary devices, to enhance your narrative and make it resonate more deeply with your audience. The risk here is falling into long-winded explanations or inauthentic feelings. I've seen students head on a traveling expedition to various countries, after which their writing spiraled into a *National Geographic*-like travel blog, only to conclude with a teary "I vow to eradicate poverty," a sentimental ending that hangs there like an appendix, adding nothing to the prose and impressing no one.

It is best to explore how your fascination with light and shadow in photography reflects your understanding of human complexity, or how a favorite book has shaped your perspective on identity and belonging. The focus is on ideas and the connections you draw rather than a traditional beginning-middle-end structure.

You can even find the intersection of two topics that fascinate you, like math and music, and examine both through the lens of what makes both the same and different.

Both styles have their strengths, and the best choice depends on your personality, experiences, and what feels most authentic to you. If you have a transformative story that highlights resilience and growth, it might be a natural fit. On the other hand, if you find yourself drawn to abstract ideas or want to paint a vivid picture of your inner world, the reflective narrative offers a canvas for creative expression.

Ultimately, what matters most is that your essay feels true to who you are. Admissions officers aren't looking for a specific type of story; they're looking for your story, told in your voice. Whether you craft a heroic journey or an introspective tapestry, trust that your unique perspective makes your essay stand out.

Essay Focus: Passion
- Public high school
- 4.2 GPA
- Accepted to a Top Ten
- Political science/journalism major

Share an essay on any topic of your choice.

Inspiration hits me after midnight. The second the clock strikes twelve, I emerge from mundane hibernation. Daytime is trivial, a mere opening act for what is to come. I yearn for the moonlight to filter through my blinds, engulfing me in pure ecstasy. Most people pour themselves a cup of coffee or chug some Red Bull, but my "energy drink" is water mixed with inspiration.

And then, I write.

Now, I am Adonia, tragically in love with my handsome Altman and desperately scheming to escape a patriarchal society that is calculated against my autonomy. I scan the surroundings of my room, fashioned with handmade silver stars, imagining that I am locked in a prison, writing a letter of last goodbyes. I am imprisoned by body and soul, and my water needs to be rationed because it will disappear quickly if I'm not careful.

Or perhaps I'm Serena, a menace that obliterates everything in her path—a wave of pure anger characterized as a human being. My hand is unusually warm, igniting a flame in its palm. The urge to light my enemies on fire and watch them burn overtakes me.

If I'm feeling particularly magical, I'm Jane, spending her last days on a beach with a man who is pure sunlight. I watch the conjury ebb and flow from Robin like the azure waves of the beach. My Lasko fan is the cool ocean breeze, and my cherry blossom comforter is a soft, warm beach towel.

Sometimes, I switch tabs between Adonia's story and a homework essay about *The Great Gatsby*, and I relish the experience of writing both. I'm as captivated by Fitzgerald's rhetorical choices as Adonia's final words to Altman.

Now, I cry. I'm solemn and silent as tears fall from my face and reach my keyboard. A sad song (specifically, the acoustic version of *Where's My Love* by SYML) blares through the speakers of my MacBook as I kill off three characters who had so much to live for. Afterward, I mull over an incident that upset me years ago and then write it out, solely for the purpose of feeling the pain all over again.

Now, I breathe. I write about how everything is too much and not enough. The way that my life is occasionally a seesaw: as something improves, another thing deteriorates. In an instant, I delete it all—the stress, the inferiority complex, and the wobbly seesaw feeling.

I remove it all, and I'm free. And then, I fill the pages with hope and wonder.

The hope and wonder that bring out all the good things that are bound to happen.

Now, I impress. I incorporate an elegant, elaborate language that will undoubtedly amaze my reader. With each word, I grow more scholarly.

I morph into a highbrow academic who reads Proust for fun instead of re-watching *Grey's Anatomy* for the millionth time. I wield my writing like colorful, vivid makeup meticulously applied to mislead those who overlook the eyeshadow and glitter that embellish my face. I parade around, smiling brightly at my judges, declaring that "I am exactly what you are looking for," and not just a girl with a MacBook Pro.

I write with the abundance of the moon, sun, and stars all at the same time.

Now, I laugh. I write a story about a boy who fails his math class, and

I proceed to giggle uncontrollably for five minutes about my unfortunate relationship with mathematics. As I rushedly finish my story, Gaps in Flight, I make a spelling mistake that shouldn't be funny, but it is—because it's three in the morning and everything is funny at three in the morning. I perform my signature dance move (the wave) when I realize that I've created a groundbreaking idea that will utterly amaze my reader.

My laptop is overheating from all the tabs I've open: research, thesaurus, and YouTube. The sky begins to pale and transitions into twilight. It's five in the morning.

And then, I sleep.

Why It Worked

This essay worked because it is deeply personal and multifaceted. The student avoids clichés, speaks in her own voice, and demonstrates her love for writing in an organic and heartfelt way. Admissions officers likely saw her as someone who would bring originality, passion, sensitivity, and a vibrant personality to their campus. Colleges value students who bring intellectual enthusiasm to their campus. This student's essay demonstrates her academic potential without explicitly listing her achievements.

The essay flows smoothly, but its most notable aspect is the enigmatic thread that runs through it. My advice is to avoid being overly cryptic or requiring the reader to work hard to understand the underlying message. Instead, focus on presenting the story in clear, accessible ways. The limit of 650 words leaves little room for suspense or ambiguity. However, in this instance, the strategy succeeded, ultimately securing her a top score and admission to one of the top ten universities in the country. Her voice is authentic and engaging. Her essay doesn't sound like a formulaic response or a mere list of accomplishments; it offers a glimpse into her thoughts and passions. The structure (moving through various moments like "Now, I write,"

"Now, I cry," etc.) adds a rhythmic and narrative quality that captivates the reader and maintains their interest.

Her work stands out with its imaginative approach and ability to transform mundane elements (such as a fan, a comforter, or a keyboard) into vivid, almost magical imagery. This essay isn't just about her love for writing; it is her writing in action. Her vivid descriptions and emotional depth demonstrate her profound connection to her craft. She demonstrates the transformative power of storytelling and reveals how it's central to her identity.

Colleges look for students with passion and intellectual curiosity, and she showcases her writing as more than a hobby; it's a way she processes life, learns, and expresses herself. This essay exhibits an element of multidimensionality, as the student doesn't limit herself to one tone or aspect of her personality. Instead, she reveals her humor, vulnerability, resilience, and ambition.

She's playful: "I giggle uncontrollably for five minutes about my unfortunate relationship with mathematics."

She's introspective: "I write about how everything is too much and not enough."

She's ambitious: "I parade around, smiling brightly at my judges, declaring that 'I am exactly what you are looking for.'"

Admissions officers gained a sense of a well-rounded person. They saw the student as self-aware and unafraid to show a multifaceted personality.

Each section flows naturally into the next, and the variations in tone (ecstatic, reflective, scholarly, humorous) keep it fresh. Instead of explicitly stating her strengths or claiming qualities like resilience, creativity, or intellect, the student demonstrates them through her narrative and descriptions.

For example, instead of saying, "I'm imaginative," she writes: "*I wield my writing like colorful, vivid makeup meticulously applied.*"

Admissions officers want to see who you are, not be told who you think you are. The use of detailed scenes and metaphors allows her to communicate her qualities compellingly.

Lastly, there are balanced, lighthearted moments, such as dancing at 3 a.m., alongside her struggles with math and serious reflections on life, identity, and creativity. This range makes her relatable and human. While the essay isn't focused on academics, her intellectual curiosity is evident through her engagement with writing, literature, and storytelling. Her description of switching between the *Great Gatsby* essay and Adonia's story subtly demonstrates her ability to balance creative and analytical thinking.

The ending ties the essay together beautifully, with the image of the sky transitioning to twilight and the line: "And then, I sleep." It's understated yet satisfying, leaving the reader with a clear sense of who she is: someone who lives and breathes creativity. A firm conclusion leaves a lasting impression.

Essay Focus: Identity
- Private high school
- 4.8 GPA
- Accepted to a Top Ten
- Major: Biomedical engineering

Some students have a background, identity, interest, or talent that is so meaningful they believe their application would be incomplete without it. If this sounds like you, then please share your story.

I see the ball hit the ground, barely reaching the boundary. It's moving low, hurtling toward my left hand, but luckily, I'm quick on my feet. I dive down in an attempt to return the shot. I feel my body hit the floor, my left hand reaching desperately for the elusive ball. I close my eyes as I feel the ball brush my fingertips, and I swing wildly toward my opponent. The shrieking sound of the bell cuts the game short and renders my last move useless. I open my eyes, eager to see the results of that point, and I'm met with the sight of a ball perched halfway up a tall bush three yards away from the court. In silence, I lock eyes with my opponent, and we laugh.

We laugh because the ball is an old tennis ball, and the court consists of merely four rectangular shapes on the concrete of our schoolyard. We laugh because the spectators are not rowdy sports fans but rather friendly colleagues who had the misfortune of being eliminated in previous rounds. We laugh because the bell is the school bell, signaling the start of the passing period, and we laugh because we are not playing a high-stakes professional sport, but a retro game of four-square at lunch.

It is unusual nowadays to see high school students at an academically driven private school running around and playing games for fun. However, every student leader aims to eliminate the formation of toxic cliques within a community, and this game of Four Square began as my way of fostering inclusivity among members of our school band. As band manager, it was my responsibility to enhance unity among our members, and a united ensemble was key to successful performances. While reflecting on how to boost camaraderie across classes and sections, I landed on the idea of a game.

While planning our annual Band Camp the summer before my junior year, I included an evening block of time for a Four Square tournament. It was a wild success. Not only was it a well-deserved break from the long hours of preparing for our marching band season, but it was also embraced by band students throughout the rest of the school year.

Soon, what had started as a bonding initiative for members of the band *program evolved into a daily lunchtime activity, engaging students from every corner of our school. Basketball stars chatted with book nerds while waiting in line, choir kids battled football players in tie-breaker lightning rounds, and upperclassmen partnered with underclassmen during our doubles games. A game I initiated to enhance bonding within the band for the upcoming season blossomed into a school tradition. Especially in the academically competitive Bay Area, creating opportunities to take a break from the demands of schoolwork and extracurricular activities has been as important to me as breaking down cliques among competitive students. In my school, it was the game of Four Square that sparked the discovery of commonalities that transcended mere appearances, fostering unlikely friendships and valuable exchanges of ideas. My band community became more unified because of my initiative to start the Four Square tradition, and eventually, the entire school was positively transformed.*

And all it took was carrying around a tennis ball in my pocket for two years.

Why It Worked

This essay has an engaging hook, vivid imagery, and light humor. This student shifts from a personal, first-person perspective to a broader, group perspective. It is an excellent example of how a simple game can be transformational and have a positive ripple effect on the group.

This personal statement feels authentic, and the use of varied sentence structures adds rhythm. This specific element of using various sentence structures is often overlooked, but it is an excellent strategy to avoid monotony and engage the reader. Just like a musician uses staccato and legato in music to portray various emotions, a skillful writer employs simple and compound sentences to achieve a memorable essay. Using grammar strategically can create effective messaging that energizes: "*I dive down in an attempt to return the shot.*" (Simple sentence, short and punchy, staccato-like.) *"I feel my body hit the floor, my left hand reaching desperately for the elusive ball."* (Compound sentence, detailed and nuanced, legato-like.) *"I close my eyes as I feel the ball brush my fingertips, and I swing wildly toward my opponent.* (Compound sentence, holds the attention on the action, slow and steady, legato-like.)

The essay effectively demonstrates key leadership qualities, including inclusivity, initiative, and strategic thinking. The writer identified a challenge (toxic cliques), envisioned a solution (the game), and executed it effectively, resulting in a lasting tradition that fostered unity and joy. The writer connects personal efforts to a broader impact, emphasizing how the game broke down barriers between diverse groups. This ability to unite people reflects a leader prioritizing community over individual gain. Organizing the Four Square game tournament required foresight, planning, and execution. The writer's decision to incorporate this into Band Camp demonstrates strategic thinking.

The ending is equally memorable: "And all it took was carrying around a tennis ball in my pocket for two years" is a concise, reflective statement that reinforces the power of small actions in creating meaningful change.

Essay Focus: Identity
- Public high school
- 3.5 GPA
- Accepted to a Top Ten
- Major: Computer science

Reflect on a time when you questioned or challenged a belief or idea. What prompted your thinking? What was the outcome?

Speak quietly, and don't argue. Wear something feminine; guests are coming. Be modest, but only talk about your successes. Nobody likes failure!

Reshma Saujani, founder of the non-profit Girls Who Code, says girls are raised to "be perfect," while boys are raised to "be brave." I agree. By far, the biggest challenge I've faced is learning how to take risks and be myself.

I'll never forget the time in 7th grade when my best friend, whom I considered my sister from another mister, managed to solve an algebra problem that nobody else could, but she refused to raise her hand out of fear that she was wrong. Furious, I began recording my classmates' behaviors. I found that although girls outnumbered boys, they answered questions less frequently. However, when they did raise their hands, they were correct more often. Until then, I'd rarely risked failure by speaking out. But I began forcing myself to answer questions without caring whether I was right. Sometimes, I'd confidently yell out answers I knew were wrong, drawing laughs. Eventually, I realized that I learned faster when I tried and missed than when I simply stayed silent. This carried over to my family life, where I stopped pretending to be flawless and began broadcasting my blunders. Not only did I feel freer, but I also grew closer to my relatives, who seemed to open as well.

"Don't be afraid to jump into the deep end of the pool," my cousin, an Apple engineer, advised me. Coincidentally, that's also how my dad had taught me to swim when I was four.

So, I dove headfirst into Hackathons, competitions in which programming teams have 24 hours to achieve a task. Although the male/female ratio is usually 10:1, I forced myself to attend my first event alone. Breathing deeply, I approached several strangers who quickly became my teammates. Our objective, to "make something involving linguistics," inspired us to design a sentiment analyzer that could learn to spot suicidal or violent tendencies in people's online postings and help avert tragedies. Amazingly, we won first place, and I've been making connections through Hackathons ever since.

Another way I've applied my burgeoning confidence is through comedy. By my freshman year, I had developed a reputation for being outspoken and possessing good-natured sarcasm. So, I joined Speech and Debate, embracing my first assignment: to perform a humorous piece called "The Iliad, The Odyssey, and all Greek Mythology in 99 Minutes or Less." It seemed funny enough until I realized I had to interpret 14 separate characters. Panicked, I leaned on advice from upper-level students, one of whom urged me to change a voice I had come up with, loosely based on the Stitch character from "Lilo & Stitch," into a Scottish accent more "typical" of competitors.

Unfortunately, my first performance fell flat. Although I'd dutifully followed recommendations, the judges appeared confused and missed half my jokes. That's when I realized that, unlike a computer following a program, a performer can't rely on instructions. By trying so hard to conform to others' conceptions of perfection, I'd buried my voice. So, for the next competition, I brought back my trademark corniness, including my orig-

inal, Stitch-inspired voice. Not only did I place fourth, but I learned another lesson about staying true to myself.

Following in Saujani's footsteps, I also began promoting females in technology at my school. I worked to get our Girls Who Code Club registered and raised awareness of our Computer Science Club by organizing fundraisers. Under my tenure as VP, we grew from a group that lacked mention in the Yearbook to a 15-member force. I led through trial and error; although we sometimes stumble, we always emerge stronger.

Despite progress, society remains replete with double standards and sexist voices. Only when I stopped listening to them did I realize I could be whoever I wanted to be and help other women do the same. Only then was I able to savor the sweetness of imperfection.

Why It Worked

The essay begins with an engaging hook: "Speak quietly, and don't argue. Wear something feminine; guests are coming. Be modest, but only talk about your successes. Nobody likes failure!"

This dramatic and culturally resonant opening grabs attention by immersing the reader in a voice shaped by societal expectations. It establishes the theme of gender norms evocatively, making the essay feel relevant and personal.

The start opens to a broader commentary. This is what I call the "funnel effect," which allows the reader to get deeper into the plot and see more of the narrator's personality. Next, the mention of Reshma Saujani's quote connects the personal struggle to a larger societal issue, signaling that the writer is self-aware and engaged in cultural conversations.

Usually, I will advise students not to use quotes. Using quotes magnifies someone else's voice, silencing your voice, which you must avoid in a personal narrative. However, we let this slide here, and there was no loss. This should serve as a reminder that, as much as there is good guidance on what to do and what not to do when writing, the rules are yours to keep and yours to break.

The essay maintains its strong narrative structure by following an almost chronological timeline. This made writing the essay easy, and the ease with which the essay reads is transferred onto the reader. The writer begins with an anecdote from seventh grade, observing gender dynamics in class. This sets the stage for the central theme: overcoming fear and embracing risk.

Phrases like "dove headfirst into Hackathons" and "confidently yell out answers I knew were wrong" add energy to the prose. The essay strikes a balance between humility and confidence, making the writer likable yet impressive.

The advice from the cousin and the childhood swimming lesson bring the essay full circle. This narrative symmetry feels intentional and satisfying.

The broader impact of this mindset shift, such as improved family relationships, demonstrates maturity and personal insight. One more element here is mentioning specific accomplishments with reflection. This works for this narrative because it supports the central premise of girl power.

If you decide to follow any of this writing structure, be careful of how you tie your story with factual achievements, since there is a bit of a danger of repeating the résumé or the activities list.

For example, the shift to the hackathon story and winning first place adds value because it is underlining the impact of these activities on the student. Ultimately, it is not what was done, but why. The why matters greatly in each story. The achievement is impressive, but what stands out is how the writer frames it: as a stepping-stone for personal growth and connection. This humility balances the narrative. The essay highlights how the writer learned to embrace failure as a path to success. This trait resonates with admissions committees looking for reflective and growth-oriented students who are unafraid to take the initiative.

Essay Focus: Personal Challenge
- Public high school
- 4.2 GPA
- Accepted Early Decision to a Top Ten
- Major: Physics/computer science

Discuss an accomplishment, event, or realization that sparked a period of personal growth and a new understanding of yourself or others.

Tenth grade was a golden age for my explorations in cooking and self. Limited by the lockdown, I turned away from my fears that my classmates would see me as inferior and unaccomplished and devoted myself to exploring the culinary arts. My approach to cooking so far has been to modify others' recipes, rather than creating from the vast expanse of possibilities. It mirrored my personality: working to improve how others see me rather than pursuing my interests. Cocooned at home with my favorite coconut pudding, I felt it was time to create from scratch, a new coconut pudding recipe and a new me.

It took me a while to decide how to approach the pudding creation without knowing the ingredients list. I first tasted this pudding at a nearby small restaurant and enjoying this delicacy had become my family's guilty pleasure. I wanted it to be perfect.

I first tried to find a recipe to use as an anchor, but all my searches yielded brownish, pasty-looking puddings, not the smooth, white, jelly-like goodness I was looking for.

After endless searching, mixing, heating, and refrigerating, my first pudding met the garbage with a "plonk," and I knew I had to change my approach. The scientist and perfectionist in me were challenged! It was a feeling I had experienced before: grinding for math competitions that no longer fulfilled me, yet I continued to do them anyway, just to be like my friends. It took me a while to abandon the extracurricular classes, AMC problems, and the Math Club. Despite the dull feeling of dissatisfaction in my heart, I pushed through it until I could no longer ignore the lack of fulfillment, at which point I quit.

Immediately after, I was left with emptiness, a time vacuum I couldn't fill. As much as I had hoped my new hobby would fill that void, and although the third trial of my cooking experiment was starting to yield some edible results, the challenge was losing its fervor. Like the many minor interests I'd been involved in, from tennis to Rubik's Cube speed solving, it felt far from what I wanted my focus to be. I realized that while cooking is excellent at improving the lives of those around me, it can't revolutionize the world as technologies can. This sharpened my focus, as I knew I wanted to work on something with a greater impact.

A month later, out of the blue, I wondered if I could get the ingredients list for the recipe from the restaurant's website. Strangely enough, there wasn't a part of me that felt unhappy about simply getting the recipe instead of inventing it. Instead, I was relieved as somewhere between trying to fill in the void from dropping math competitions and perfecting the scientific method through recipes, I had spent many hours reading Feynman and taking online classes and found my true passion—physics. It felt intuitive and logically connected, perhaps because many of the principles of physics are a statement of our natural intuition in a precise, quantitative way. Moreover, compared to my years with math, learning physics felt effortless; I didn't need an extracurricular class to give assignments or a looming competition date to drive me to learn more.

Eventually, I had to learn calculus to better understand physics, so I reluctantly joined an MITx calculus class. To my surprise, calculus was highly interesting, and I finally appreciated the beauty of math that I couldn't see when I was buried too deep in the minutiae of math. While taking the class, school had resumed, and compared to last year, I felt relaxed and confident. The old insecurity that the talents and accomplishments of others may be greater than my own had vanished, because I felt pretty happy to work on my interest in physics. But, of course, if ever my best isn't as good as others, I can always pull out a smooth, white, jelly-like goodness and call it a day.

Why It Worked

The strong visuals draw the reader in, and it is evident that true fulfillment for this student comes from following intrinsic interests, not from pleasing others.

This belief guides the entire essay, from cooking to math competitions to discovering physics. The references this student makes are not random; every story, failure, and realization ties back to this personal truth: "I must work from passion, not pressure."

The best personal statements are not about listing achievements; they're about revealing the evolution of thinking, which this one does perfectly.

The student is honest about the cooking disaster, which unfolds as a failed science experiment, and the emptiness felt before quitting math competitions. The feelings of self-doubt and inferiority are raw and authentic. This vulnerability builds immediate trust with the reader. Admissions officers are tired of fake "perfect" essays; they want to see growth, struggle, failure, and genuine personality.

This essay feels like a conversation, not a résumé. It demonstrates emotional resilience rather than boasting about it.

Another element worth noting is the symbolism. The coconut

pudding is a genius literary device here because it's playful and sensory (smell, taste, texture); it symbolizes the journey of trial, error, and discovery; and it recurs subtly at the end ("smooth, white, jelly-like goodness"), satisfyingly tying the essay together.

The story never feels like "and then ... and then ... and then ..." As each scene ends, the reader is brought back to the coconut pudding metaphor, hinting at a much deeper philosophical maturity. Every event, along with the personal growth it prompts, leads to the next, creating a smooth flow rather than a checklist-like sequence.

The essay's ending revisits the original pain point, but now we view the author in a new light, filled with optimism and determination: "... if ever my best isn't as good as others, I can always pull out a smooth, white, jelly-like goodness and call it a day."

Essay Focus: Personal Challenges
- Private high school
- 4.8 GPA
- Accepted Early Decision to a Top Ten
- Major: Computer science

Discuss an accomplishment, event, or realization that sparked a period of personal growth and a new understanding of yourself or others.

I was bored with gravity. I was over the constant ache in my back from standing. I grew tired of the way my feet hurt after I ran. I was tired of being grounded. I wanted to fly.

So, I started diving to escape the physical burdens of existing on land (while also looking like a star).

There is one particular aspect of diving that messes with my mind: inward flips. Theoretically, they seem simple—stand backward on the board, jump, and rotate forward one full rotation. In practice, it's a different story. Standing on the board before an inward flip feels like a fight against every rational cell in my body screaming, "DON'T JUMP."

One chilly March afternoon, as I prepared myself for an inward flip, I was faced with a choice: to give in to the utterly paralyzing fear of hitting the board, or to trust in my abilities and fly. My mind was quiet, but my body was alert. Millions of icy raindrops raced down my back. The bleachers creaked under the weight of the crowd of spectators; their eyes burrowed holes into my body. My ankles began to move, gently rocking the board, building momentum for the final jump. The sounds of the world around me intensified, giving way to the silence of everyone collectively holding their breath as I prepared to jump. It was my time to fly.

Yet in the next moment, I felt the rough edge of the board with only one of my feet. Just a slight, insignificant turn of the hips, and my leg just barely missed the end of the board. My other knee buckled under the added strain. I found myself on my back in the water, sinking deeper into the cold embrace of the pool.

I did not fly. It was only after I pulled myself out of the pool that I could see the blood seeping from my right foot, leaving a small trail of red puddles in my path, which were immediately swept away by the rain.

"Do you want to continue?" someone asked.

No voice, nothing, came out of me. I felt a primal impulse to flee, to set the ground ablaze behind me, to leave my mistake deep under the water, where it had first hit me: I had fallen. My dive attempt was over before it began.

Watching the blood weep out of my foot, I felt every impulse to run away melt from my mind. I needed to get back on the boards. I needed to prove to everyone that I am not defined by one mistake, to prove to myself that I am more than my failures.

I found my voice. "Absolutely."

I carry the scar from this experience with me to this day. Every time I dive, I can see it snaking around the side of my foot, reminding me that falling is just another part of life—how I get up defines who I am.

Two weeks after this experience, I stepped onto a different set of boards, ready to attempt the same dive: an inward flip. I looked down at my feet to calm my jangled nerves, catching a glimpse of the end of the scar I knew crossed the bottom of my right heel. I took an extra second to reconsider the choice before me: fly or fall?

But before the second was over, I was already in the air, heading toward a successful and high-scoring inward flip. As I let the water slow my descent into the vast expanse of the pool, I knew I had flown.

Why It Worked

The essay has a compelling opening hook: "I was bored with gravity." It is original, emotional, and immediately grabs attention. It establishes a clear personal motivation—to escape physical limits. The sensory details describing the moments before the jump create vivid imagery: "Millions of icy raindrops ran races down my back." The physical tension before the jump is intense and cinematic, leading to a clear emotional arc. Fear of failure transforms into determination and ultimately redemption; this structure is very satisfying.

Admissions officers favor resilience stories, and this one feels genuine, even though writing about sports, injuries, and competitions is a common theme. What makes this one stand out is the emotional depth and personal reflection that elevate it beyond the typical "overcame adversity on the field" narrative. The scar becomes a personal symbol of persistence, connecting the experience to the final victory in a powerful, symbolic way.

There are a few sentences that are a bit overwritten. "The bleachers creaked under the weight of the crowd of spectators; their eyes burrowed holes into my body" is a strong image, but slightly overpacked. Importantly, however, the essay concludes with internal growth, not external validation: "I knew I had flown." Again, this is a confident and emotional ending.

CHAPTER 15

School-Specific Essays: How to Approach the "Why Us?" Essay

> THE SUPPLEMENTAL ESSAYS ARE WHERE YOU EXPERTLY COMBINE A RÉSUMÉ, IDENTITY, AND A REASON.

The supplemental essays specific to each college might feel like an afterthought, but do not underestimate their importance. Even if the college has labeled them as "optional," make no mistake, they will read and review them diligently.

In particular, the "Why Us?" essay is trickier than it seems. You need to find the intersection between the school and your passions, personality, and aspirations. The school specifically asks you to explain why you have chosen them among the numerous other colleges and universities. This requires an understanding of what they offer, their culture, and, most importantly, who you are. Take your time; research the school thoroughly and visit if possible. Nothing beats having a firsthand account of the lay of the land. Many visits lead to personal anecdotes that students later weave into their essays, which is a big plus for uniqueness (instead of copying text from the website like most do) and demonstrating genuine interest at the same time.

Here are two NYU-specific essays written by different students to allow you to compare. The prompt for both was "Why NYU?" and both students were accepted.

Crowded streets of rushing people, traffic gridlocks, numbers flying on the screen of the stock exchange ... The Big Apple! I feel invigorated, limitless, and free; I am at home. My taxi stops at West 4th and Green Street. Here, in the heart of the city, is NYU. Pulsing with unlimited opportunities, spreading its intellectual prowess far and wide to all continents, is a campus with no walls and no gates. Coming face-to-face with the infamous Greenwich Village, I am humbled but impatient. I see my dreams and goals realized here: the ability to acquire the essential business fundamentals to affect social change on a global scale.

The flexibility and freedom to major in business at NYU Stern, with concentrations in Finance, Global Business, and Computing and Data Science, is my greatest desire. Additionally, I strive to gain essential technical skills by pursuing a minor in Computer Science from NYU Tandon, combined with an Advanced Mathematical Methods minor from the top-ranked NYU Courant. This impeccable combination of highly renowned institutions will afford me the highest quality of education.

Throughout my undergraduate studies, I would study in London to witness first-hand the unfolding of events such as Brexit, in Shanghai to better understand the Chinese economy and its adverse impact on the US economy, and in New York, as the world's premier financial center. I will immerse myself in ethnic environments that will expand my intellectual mindset and help me internalize how global economies interact.

NYU is home to world-renowned faculty and industry professionals who offer world-class economic perspectives. Nobel Laureate Professor A. Michael Spence and his work on economic policies in emerging markets would allow me to apply that knowledge globally. I learned about the ARCH model from Nobel Laureate Robert Engle, which is currently used to forecast volatility in various economic analyses, such as stock prices, GDP, and interest rates, thereby helping to minimize the risks involved in international banking. Understanding Professor Engle's model will significantly help me predict different trends as I aspire to become an investment banker and a successful entrepreneur.

I look forward to utilizing the NYU Startup Hub and Stern Venture Fellows, gaining access to advising, seed funding, and workshops to launch my future entrepreneurial projects.

As Frank Sinatra sang it in his signature song, "I want to wake up in the city that never sleeps."

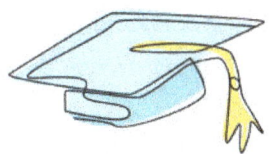

The Big Apple hits me like an old quintessential jazz piece. I follow the strong meter, obey the distinctive tone, and move in rhythm with the patterns. The mystical energy of Greenwich Village instantly draws me. Any direction I turn, I feel its highs and lows; it's a jazz fusion of sounds and sights, improvising at every street corner. I claim my space on the busy street and pause to marvel at the sight of NYU—an institution "without walls" brimming with students worldwide. This is the life I have always imagined after high school.

At New York University, I envision myself majoring in Neuroscience at the College of Arts and Sciences. Ever since my freshman year of high school, I have been heavily involved in the world of Alzheimer's and dementia. Having worked in a dementia-specialized senior care home and closely with the Alzheimer's Association, I know the devastating effects Alzheimer's can have on people. I began exploring and writing for my scientific research on the topic of neuroplasticity and brain health, and I took part in every experiment in my AP Psychology class; however, the more I read, the more unanswered questions mounted in my head. How can we better understand the connection between music and Alzheimer's Disease?

Pursuing Neuroscience at New York University will allow me to explore this disease in conjunction with my other passion, jazz music, under the mentorship of some of the world's finest faculty. In fact, it was NYU's Dr. Thomas Wisniewski who inspired me to continue my journey in neuroscience when I read his work during my sophomore year. His paper on using localized proteomics to identify pathogenesis in Alzheimer's disease fascinates me even today. I am constantly wowed by the work conducted at the Alzheimer's Disease Center at the Langone Center of Cognitive Neurology, and I am confident that I can learn and provide my personal experiences by working with Alzheimer's patients one day.

At NYU, I will attend the Joint Neuroscience Colloquia seminars to experience the association with distinguished speakers from around the world. I would attend the annual CNC symposium on neuroscience and collaborate with scholars from NYU's renowned lab to update my knowledge and further my pursuits in neuroscience. NYU is a place of many opportunities for me, a place I consider to be the most extraordinary combination of misfits, abstract thinkers, and visionaries who come together to change the world. And I know that I have my place among them.

SCHOOL SPECIFIC ESSAYS: HOW TO APPROACH THE "WHY US?" ESSAY

The 'Why Us?' college-specific essay is not unique to NYU. When you begin to write a "Why Us?" essay, you're not just answering why you like a school, but showing why you and the school are a great match. How will you make the most of the facilities and curriculum? Will you naturally fit into the culture the school has built? That's what colleges and universities expect from their students. The supplemental essay is a short persuasive piece where the goal is to make an admissions officer nod and say, "Yes, I can see this student here."

The best place to start is with a hook that's personal and specific. You need an opening that clearly shows this essay could only be written for this college. The question "Why Us?" actually asks why us among the many schools in the same area, city, and state. This is where your knowledge of the school's unique qualities and offerings will come into play. It could be a moment you experienced during a campus visit, a detail you noticed in a virtual tour, or an academic connection that caught your attention while researching the school. Maybe you remember standing in a glass-walled robotics lab watching students debate how to reduce errors in a machine you'd only read about in textbooks, or you came across a professor's research paper and recognized the same curiosity that's kept you coding after midnight.

Every college has its special feature.

I visit many colleges each year, and I can confidently say that even the smell inside the lecture halls differs at Stanford compared to other Northern California colleges. There's a cool, musty calm in the air, the kind of scent that seems to have settled over decades of discussion and thought. When you step outside, you see rose bushes lining the walkways, ivy quietly curling along the walls. Inside, the air remains still and controlled, contrasting with the bright California sunlight. These are more than just classrooms; it feels like a place where time slows down, where the noise from the outside world can't quite reach you, and your mind is free to open and expand.

Start your supplemental essay with an engaging hook, then promptly introduce your thesis—a sentence that clearly states why you're applying and what you hope to contribute. Here, you should outline both sides of the relationship: what you want to gain from the school and what the school will gain from you. For example, you might say you want to deepen your research in cognitive psychology while also helping to expand mental health programming on campus. You could mention that the school's specific lab facilities and peer mentorship network make it the ideal place to pursue both goals.

From there, your job is to support your claim with evidence. Be cautious of turning this into a list of generic qualities, like mentioning the beautiful campus and great reputation. Anyone can say those, and they could apply to many schools. Instead, select two or three specific, well-researched details and connect each one to your personal background or future goals. If you're interested in public policy, you might mention a speaker series that allows interaction with policymakers, a student organization that aligns with your previous work, and the benefit of being in a city where policy is made in real time. Each reason should feel like part of your personal plan, not just a fact from the school's homepage.

Once you've provided those specifics, reflect on them yourself. Remind the reader how these opportunities connect to the work you've already begun and the challenges you're eager to face. This is your chance to demonstrate that you're not just a consumer of what they offer, but you will be an active contributor. You want them to see that you'll arrive on campus prepared to participate, lead, and create.

End by looking forward. Give them an image of you in motion at their school: walking across the quad to a meeting you've been preparing for all week, sitting in the lab you once only read about, or standing at the microphone in a student forum. The more they can picture you there, the stronger the connection between your story and their campus will feel.

And above all, remember the test: If you can replace the school's name with another and the essay still works, it's too generic. This is your chance to mirror the school's values and offerings while anchoring them in your own history, goals, and voice, making it clear that you don't just want to attend, you belong there. Here's how Columbia University has given the same prompt a new flavor:

Please tell us what you value most about Columbia and why.

My inner nerd gleams, stepping into Math Club every Tuesday. It's the best place for me to hang out, train for competitions, and make the stupidest jokes known to mankind. It gets better once the abstract equations are taken off the page, sent to the real world with the power of Computer Science. Cliché as it sounds, I got the bug from my computer scientist dad. It all started the day I visited his office. Tall for a first-grader, I stood in front of the sleek, gargantuan monitors. They were nothing like the triangle Macintoshes at school. I was welcomed into the future, but the problem was that I had no idea what was going on. I was the "curious cat", but leashed so nothing goes sideways.

You know that blend of feelings when you're nervous and excited? Too scared to make a move but too curious not to. I had it during my first Python course, Computer Science Club meetings, and AP Computer Science class, but I still have a long way to go. I learn about innovations but understanding the intricacies are beyond my reach. I would explore the endless possibilities of Artificial Intelligence and Machine Learning, leveraging my passion for math within the avant-garde Student Research Program. Today's technology allows Artificial Intelligence to do anything from mastering Go to understanding digital media, like how relationships between social media, news, and the economy are understood using graphs, according to a 2015 report by Columbia's Data Science Institute. On a much larger scale, Artificial Intelligence might one day help avert a terrorist attack or save civilians during a natural disaster. I might be a rookie, but I know I value curiosity the way Columbia values exploration, relentlessly. I want to merge my love of math with cutting-edge research through Columbia's Student Research Program, tackling problems that have no answer in the back of a book. Surrounded by the innovation hubs of Facebook and Amazon, Columbia isn't just a school for me, but it's a launchpad.

The following prompt asking about the world you come from is a favorite among many colleges. It looks deceptively simple, and even though you might be tempted to give a full description of your town, school, or club, this essay is less about geographical location and activities and more about the fingerprints they have left on you. Examine how these two students use specific moments to reveal background and identity in motion:

Describe the world you come from; for example, your family, clubs, school, community, city, or town. How has that world shaped your dreams and aspirations?

Until middle school, I was introverted and socially awkward. I remember feeling crushed when I learned my peers had participated in a robot competition without me. Not only did the lost opportunity motivate me to change, but it also made me determined not to let the same fate befall my brother.

Five years my junior, my brother shares my computer science-loving genes. By second grade, he was building Lego cars and airplanes. When I first showed him a video of a robot, his eyes lit up. He recruited some classmates, and Team Whizbots was soon preparing for its FIRST Lego

League Junior Competition. That year's challenge, "Disaster Blaster," was to design a solution related to natural disasters. Over the next few months, I coached the seven-year-olds on the principles of stable, earthquake-ready buildings and bridges. Our working model of an earthquake simulator and robot won first in the newbies' category. Five years later, Rushil is still with Whizbots, preparing for regionals.

In many ways, my brother and I are opposites. He struggles with physical activities while I build shelves and do household repairs. Yet, I'm in awe of his mental strength and speed. He has many more friends than I did at his age, partly because I've encouraged him to be social. The years between us disappear when we're confiding in each other about our problems or bonding over technology and movies. In college and beyond, I'd continue creating lasting bonds, encouraging everyone I care about to live without regrets.

Throughout my life, I have been taught to appreciate knowledge and value it as another vital organ. Often, it was little things: my grandfather translated the labels on my favorite Japanese snacks despite having no Japanese ancestry. My father unraveled the world of computers under the milky lights of Fry's stores. My mother taught me the perfect peppercorn-to-oil ratio for stir-fries.

I've grown up investigating, from wiring a circuit board to constructing an eclipse viewer. But for a long time, I hated what knowledge seemingly equated to: afternoons drenched with grammar practice rather than the chatter of friends. Yet every time I whined, I was reminded that my family has confronted challenges in the name of education for generations.

My parents immigrated to the U.S., determined to learn in a free world. My father had learned from the lessons of my grandfather, who, during the Chinese Cultural Revolution, had been forced to set aside college to farm. He spent four years pursuing his doctorate in Japan, completing his Ph.D. at the age of 48. Throughout those years, he was separated from his young son but learned the language he would someday use to translate snack labels for his granddaughter.

When this tale finally resonated with me, I became aware of the frailty of learning and determined to pursue it as ardently as my ancestors had. They've taught me to appreciate questions, and I want to ask and answer them forever. It runs in my blood.

Your identity wouldn't be complete without one more piece of evidence: your choice of major. At first glance, this might seem like a shift in focus, almost as if the colleges are changing the subject and finally asking you to discuss something concrete, like what you plan to study. But these prompts are far from casual. In fact, they're skillfully designed, the kind of question a keen detective would ask to confirm a theory.

Admissions officers use these essays to test for alignment: Does the story you've told about yourself hold up when asked about your intellectual interests? Do your passions, pursuits, and proposed central idea connect in a way that feels consistent, curious, and real? These essays are your chance to establish this consistency without falling into the trap of describing your interest in a specific major by using your activities, like in a résumé. The two examples that follow avoid this by focusing on the meaning of the role, rather than just the role itself.

Pick what field of study at MIT appeals to you the most right now, and tell us more about why this field of study appeals to you.

I want to study computation and cognition at MIT to solve cognitive decline. Lao nian chi dai, or Alzheimer's disease, is a phrase used casually in my household when someone forgets something. We say it lightheartedly: fortunate to have never been affected by Alzheimer's. But the phrase's implications scare me.

I want to understand how the brain absorbs and loses knowledge, and I believe that artificial intelligence and machine learning have the power to tackle this complex comprehension. Through MIT's unique interdisciplinary study program, I'll have the opportunity to simultaneously study the matrix of computation and the intricacies of the brain.

I call 3 AM my golden hour. That's when I get the most genius startup ideas. More importantly, at 3:01 AM PST, I receive the treasured MIT Daily newsletter and, on Sundays, the MIT Weekly. It's the best spontaneous subscription I made at the start of my freshman year. This has become the most invigorating part of my day, and I earnestly read every section, every research article, and every Q&A of each MIT Daily during the hour-long drive to school, starting with the urban studies section.

Inadvertently, I had spent much time diving into this previously unknown territory, and I found a puzzle piece tucked under my fists, which was the connection to healthcare. While MIT's carbon nanotubes and Chicago's urban boxes on traffic lights sounded revolutionary, my 14-year-old self was more captivated by the relation to healthcare. That's how the Mobile Urban Sensing System was born. I am part of the monumental work I read about daily by majoring in urban science and planning, with a focus on computer science, particularly in the areas of health and innovation.

The following prompt asks how you've brought people together, mediated conflicts, or contributed to a group. At places like MIT, where every applicant is a high performer, the real question is: Are you compassionate? Can you lift others without needing the spotlight? The best responses show humility and a clear understanding of what it takes to move a group toward a shared goal, and exemplify academic brilliance with values.

At MIT, we bring people together to better the lives of others. MIT students work to improve their communities in different ways, from tackling the world's biggest challenges to being good friends. Describe one way in which you have contributed to your community, whether in your family, the classroom, your neighborhood, etc.

As my digital pencil finishes the last swoop, I soak in the crisp, clean logo I've created for Stanford's Stat4Onc conference. The countless hours and drafts spent finding the perfect balance between colors and shapes were worth it. With a family history of cancer, I volunteered my services as a graphic designer, hoping that my design would entice thousands of people to learn the importance of statistical oncology research.

After drawing for years, I started digital design in eighth grade when a local preschool asked, after seeing my art online, if I could create their yearbook cover.

Although scared of messing up with a foreign medium, I fell in love with graphic design as I learned the intricacies of layers and color filling on my iPad.

Since then, many organizations have enlisted my design skills. My conference logo for the Bay Area Biotech-Pharma Statistical Workshop graced banners, tote bags, and conference halls, while my clear-cut website connected community members with the event. Closer to home, I developed a minimalistic logo for my father's startup and promotional materi-

als for a high school economics initiative.

For a long time, I didn't think of my work as more than pretty resting points for random eyes, but as I reflected, I saw that I had distilled information, appealed to audiences, and leveraged unique brand styles. With a tablet and pen, I've woven myself into the beautiful haven of passions and people around me.

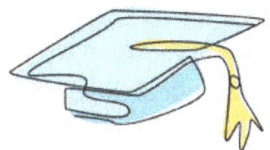

I'm most definitely not a friend of spiders, but for description purposes, I'm afraid I'll have to compare myself to one. Imagine the web as threads that connect each purpose, each story, and everyone. Throughout high school, I networked and formed mini webs of interconnected threads.

I began with Stanford's Women in Data Science (WiDS) initiative. Here, a team of six undergraduates and I develop data science guides and Python notebooks for teachers worldwide, including those in my hometown, in India, and Tanzania. We organize speaker events and empower girls to become future "feminists." However, my contributions to WiDS stemmed from our team's challenges during the ongoing COVID-19 pandemic, as we were limited in our ability to test the guides and perform general outreach. In response, I developed a WiDS outreach initiative, which involved establishing high school branches internationally.

The first step I took was connecting my web. As the Director of Health Technologies, I brought together my ScienceConnect team, which had contacts with high school clubs in the Bay Area and Boston, to advertise our international coding competition. To test our crafted guides on high *schoolers, I currently incorporate WiDS into my school's AI4Healthcare club as the president and witness the inspiring results of our work.*

From ScienceConnect, AI4Healthcare, and now to Sacred Heart, the center where I've tutored low-income students for 6 years, I envision a synchronous working space with the WiDS team and the community. In doing so, I guess you can call me your friendly neighborhood Spider-Woman.

Colleges recognize that students are busy, so you might wonder how these supplemental essays are related to anything important or relevant to your future college life. What they are really asking is: How do you really spend your time when no one is watching or giving you direction? Time is a precious commodity, and how you choose to spend it reveals a great deal about your values. What are your priorities? The strongest responses will not be forced or trying to impress. You can share how you recharge, and this is where you can give them a glimpse of a "day in the life" of being your usual teen self.

Here are two examples:

We know you lead a busy life full of activities, many of which are required of you. Tell us about something you do simply for the pleasure of it.

My zodiac sign horoscope tells me I find it hard to unburden my emotions. Most of my chart is freakishly accurate, but the horoscope fails to recognize that such emotion is unveiled through a different outlet. For me, that is music: Carnatic Indian vocal music. Since the age of 3, I would practice for hours after a weekly class, and soon became proficient enough to hear any song once and replicate the exact tune, regardless of the genre. But then, I grew up. What was once natural has now become an entirely new subject—mathematics. Before calculus, I found counting the number of orangutans or basketballs uninspiring. Music convinced me otherwise. The advanced level of Indian vocals was more than just improvising complex notes upon demand. The notes followed a microtone, aligned with the accompanying percussionists, and ended exactly on the beat. If a tune was 32 notes, I had to improvise nine patterns of 3, pause, and pick up a catchy five-note ending, all while using my hands to maintain tempo. Approximately 100 tasks involving the frontal lobe for pattern recognition, prediction, and calculation, the hippocampus for memory, and the motor cortex for hand movement were running simultaneously. Inadvertently, I'd encoded an algorithm in my brain that showed my hands and voice where and when to start and end. Executed with ease and melody, music took its shape in a meaningful string of patterns and calculations. The different lines talked to me in such a way that I'd imagine the 26 orangutans meeting 5 lions in 3rd-grade math problems, and soon, the complex calculations in my mind looked a lot like my convolutional neural networks filled with meaning.

In my brother's bento box, I begin my sunset painting. Pale yellow egg rolls, filled with pork sung, are arranged in a row, like dominoes, as a backdrop. A dollop of potato salad in the corner becomes the shining Sun, radiating with pickled white cabbage strips. On the far end, I form a kaleidoscopic pattern of lavender with lotus root circles. Splashes of marigold carrot slices fill in the remaining gaps.

As I take in the perfectly fitting pieces of my creation, a burst of satisfaction floods me. I carefully pack the container into my brother's lunch bag as the clock strikes 7:00 a.m.

With a passion for beautifying everything, my ability to create art from mundane food always enthralls me. The first time I saw a Japanese bento on YouTube, it had onigiri rice balls compacted together to form teddy bears. I was mesmerized by the miniature shapes, which appeared like delicious puzzles oozing with possibilities of what I might build. Crafting these intricate compositions became a soothing and scrumptious form of love, appealing to my aesthetics and guaranteeing that no matter what my brother encountered at school, he would have a lunch packed with care.

As he dashes in at the end of the day, eagerly displaying his empty bento, I can hardly wait for the next morning of cooking. And when he walks out the door the next day, I yell after him to carry his lunch carefully so as not to disturb its delicate assembly.

However, not all college essays include obvious keywords like "major" or "career." Some prompts are more flexible by offering larger word limits or open-ended questions, such as this one: *"Please share any additional information not included in the application that will help us get to know you better."*

Don't be fooled. These open-ended invitations are just as intentional. They give you the freedom to complete the picture, but they still serve as a final test of self-awareness: Will you use this space to reinforce your narrative, reveal your intellectual curiosity, or sense of humor, or show a unique hobby? There's always more to a person than what fits into checkboxes and word counts, even if the essay prompt is open-ended and open to interpretation:

Please share any additional information not included in the application that will help us get to know you better.

I have always desired to have my garden. Watching the rosemary bushes outside our condo grow and blossom made me sick with longing for my own piece of land. I wanted to grow not flowers and shrubs but something that would feed me and my family. One day, I finally convinced my dad, and he bought a giant pot that took a few burly men from Home Depot to bring it to our house, and I planted my first plant—a tomato. To my excitement, the vine grew like the beanstalk from the Jack and the Beanstalk fairy tale, and pretty soon, we had a tomato infestation. The problem now became how to feed the entire neighborhood with tomatoes fast enough so we could utilize them all.

As my tomato vine continued to flourish, I couldn't help but feel a sense of accomplishment. It was as if I had stumbled upon a secret formula for growing the largest, juiciest tomatoes in town. The vine stretched and climbed, reaching heights that seemed impossible for a humble tomato plant.

But as the days passed, our once serene suburban street transformed into a tomato frenzy. Neighbors, friends, and even strangers from the next block over started showing up at our doorstep, all with the same tomato-obsessed look in their eyes.

My dad, initially supportive of my gardening dream, now found himself in a tomato conundrum of epic proportions. We had more tomatoes than we knew what to do with. Our kitchen countertops were overflowing, and our fridge was bursting at the seams with ripe, red orbs of goodness.

I couldn't bear to see the surplus tomatoes go to waste, so I embarked on a mission to feed the entire neighborhood. It was like a tomato-themed superhero saga, with me as the Tomato Avenger, armed with recipes for tomato sauce, salsa, and gazpacho.

Word quickly spread, and soon, our neighbors were coming over for impromptu tomato-themed gatherings. Tomato fights became a regular occurrence, and kids in the neighborhood started using tomatoes instead of baseballs.

As summer turned to fall, we hosted the "Great Tomato Festival," complete with tomato-themed games, contests for the largest tomato, and even a tomato toss. It was a tomato extravaganza unlike anything our neighborhood had ever seen. Through it all, my desire for a garden had unintentionally transformed our community. We went from a quiet street to a tomato-loving neighborhood, bonded by the love of these red gems. And while I never imagined my first tomato plant would lead to a tomato takeover, I wouldn't have had it any other way.

So, if you ever find yourself longing for a garden, remember that sometimes, your dreams can grow beyond your wildest expectations—even if it means sharing your harvest with the entire neighborhood.

After showcasing intellectual curiosity through academics, it is time to raise the stakes. This prompt expects vulnerability and self-reflection. Don't over-dramatize or underplay hardship. The following examples strike a balance between the two.

Tell us about the most significant challenge you've faced or something important that didn't go according to plan. How did you manage the situation?

I experience the phenomenon I call "the anticipation of the red bubble." I recall praying that a red "1" bubble would appear at the corner of the mail desktop icon. Perhaps, a Nigerian prince had decided I was worthy of financing his investment funds. I began to investigate the root cause of my unusual addiction to email responses. I had an abundance of ideas and questions, but I was the child outside a candy shop, grasping for answers in vain (just within reach?) through the form of emailing. A year later, no responses formed a beautiful friendship between me and Google. I managed to give birth to some of my ideas in my "ideas book" and theorized prototypes. As much as I convinced myself into thinking a complete product with a potential global impact was achievable, I knew that my bounds were limited without expert eyes. The struggle to find a perfect mentor reflected the inadequacies of my projects, but I nevertheless continued generating new topics and prototypes to aid various problems. Despite the significant progress I was making, my questions remained unanswered, and I was speeding through research papers with blatant knowledge gaps. I realized I was asking all the right questions to all the wrong sources, and that finding a suitable mentor wasn't as easy as "Open Sesame!" I didn't give up, and as I continued learning from my projects, a red bubble finally appeared in the form of an internship. Although my request for a project mentor fell short, my whole high school motto of "smart technologies" will come to a beautiful close as graduation approaches. I wait for a red bubble from MIT so that no idea, no question, no prototype would be left behind.

For almost a decade, the ebb and flow of Chinese dance nourished me.

To the twinkling of harps and drums, I glided across stages in tightly knit formations like a peacock, eagle, or bamboo maiden. Like raindrops in a pond, my steps fell alongside those of the girls around me to form a beautiful pattern. I wanted to stay in the perfect etching of our formations forever.

But before middle school, my parents decided that I would quit. Long practices, competitions, and costly costumes were impractical, they said. I remember the hot, angry tears pouring down my face like it was yesterday.

As others lived my dream, I felt empty and abandoned. Externally, I shut out mentions of dance, but inside, I was desperate for something that could give me the same feeling. When my parents implored me to consider the possibility of drawing, I reluctantly agreed to make a visit to an art studio.

At first, my strokes were harsh and angry as I tried to conquer the paper. But when the fury subsided, a rhythm appeared. My hands stroked across the paper, chiseling out a sphere inch by inch. When everything was woven together, and I perceived the smooth ball I had rendered, I felt the same joy that had consumed me under the stage lights.

Nourished by a lost love, art has blossomed in the prior vacancy of my heart. Having braved rage and sadness, its roots today are stronger than ever.

Colleges care about your passion, and the prompt about passion and hobbies is often combined into a single, lengthy question covering multiple topics. The example here shows how to approach such a prompt. However, if your prompt includes everything—passion, hobbies, talents, interests, or skills—you can choose the one most relevant to your story. Remember that admissions officers mainly want to see how invested you are and if you care enough about a topic to put in effort. Passion is what ignites a fire and builds a bridge. The real power comes from making connections between what sparks your interest and how that spark crosses disciplines and experiences. Whether the passion is for mathematics, music, fashion, or coding, the essay needs to do more than just name it. Many essays fall short here; they describe a hobby or subject but forget that passion without follow-through is superficial. In the following essay, the student explains how they took a leap to turn an interest into a passion.

Demonstrate your passion in and out of the classroom and why you have selected this major.

After watching YouTube videos on how neural networks conceptually work, I became curious about how those ideas were implemented in code. So, I challenged myself to create a machine learning program in Python without using any machine learning packages or libraries (like TensorFlow, PyTorch, etc.). The model needed to perform three basic functions: 1. Calculating node activation values from a set of inputs. 2. Implementing the backpropagation algorithm, which uses the node values calculated previously to find the gradient of the cost function (how inaccurate the model is). Finally, applying the gradient descent algorithm to improve the model by adjusting its weights and biases based on the gradient. For each part of the model, I utilized NumPy's vectorized linear algebra methods whenever possible. It was quite challenging and enjoyable to discover how to correctly multiply the weight and bias matrices with the node value vectors to obtain the right results. After a month of planning, writing, and debugging, I finally finished, and I trained it on the MNIST dataset to see if it could recognize handwritten numbers.

Of course, it didn't work perfectly the first time; the activation function I'd used was the logistic function, so the cost function gradients were minimal, resulting in the model learning extremely slowly. I searched online and found a variety of activation functions I could use, so I modified my model to allow the user to specify the activation function each layer uses.

I wanted to apply my model to clean energy, as I had heard that machine learning has many applications in the field, particularly in predicting electricity demand and renewable energy sources. I entered a Kaggle competition using smart meter data to identify buildings consuming anomalously high amounts of energy. It wasn't as simple as directly plugging in the input data. I had to modify the given data due to some overflow errors and downsample the training set to a 1:1 ratio of anomalies to non-anomalies, as anomalies were extremely rare in the provided training data. In the end, my model achieved a 70% accuracy rate on the test dataset using the meter reading, square footage, year the building was built, # of floors, air temperature, and the time of the reading as inputs.

Every year, colleges review their supplemental essay prompts, revising or rephrasing them to better reflect their evolving priorities and the qualities they seek in applicants. Although most questions stay similar in nature, in recent years, I've noticed selective schools like USC, for example, introducing questions that don't ask about the student's academic achievements or personality; instead, they assess the breadth of their thinking, social awareness, and ability to frame a global issue within a broader human context.

If you are targeting schools, especially those with strong engineering programs, use questions like this to position yourself as a problem solver who thinks beyond your own needs and into the realm of societal impact. Make it clear that you understand the complexity and urgency of a global challenge and can articulate a clear priority and defend it.

Engineering, in its fundamental nature, is about solving real-world problems, and as a future professional, you will be expected to connect technical innovation to human well-being.

This is primarily a values and vision question, quite different from the "Why Us?" or "What Major?" questions. In this case, a strong response highlights you as a student who is both technically skilled and socially aware, two qualities highly valued by colleges.

The difficulty in answering this kind of prompt comes from expertly connecting clear priorities and global context without overly generalizing (so be sure to research and read on the matter beforehand) and avoiding sounding like you are writing an informed opinion piece. Establishing a personal connection with a global issue of massive proportions, like global warming, deforestation, clean water, universal health, or any such issue, is not easy. Once finished, read your work out loud and evaluate your analysis of the problem and your solutions. Suggesting surface-level solutions, for example, "Providing resources in the form of education and specialists," can be a starting point, but it's vague; go deeper into specific technologies or strategies, which will require some reading and knowledge on your part.

While the world as a whole may be more technologically advanced than ever before, the National Academy of Engineering (NAE) has outlined 14 Grand Challenges

that engineers should focus on to improve life on the planet. You can learn about the Grand Challenges at www.engineeringchallenges.org and tell us which challenge is most important and why.

Providing access to clean water is the most critical of the Grand Challenges. More than 2.2 billion people worldwide lack access to safely managed drinking water, according to the WHO, and the consequences are not theoretical; they include children missing school due to waterborne illnesses, families walking miles for daily supplies, and entire regions unable to develop economically.

Fresh water on Earth is limited and can be recycled, but our past and current mismanagement, pollution, overuse, and uneven distribution have decreased its availability. Climate change worsens the issue, as droughts become more severe and weather patterns change, making water scarcity a daily challenge for millions. In developing countries, the distance to clean water is not just about convenience; it's a matter of life and death.

I saw this firsthand when I visited family in rural India two summers ago. Each morning, before sunrise, my cousin would walk half a mile to a community pump that often ran dry by midday. It was a striking contrast to my life in the U.S., where turning on a faucet was a thoughtless act. That experience crystallized for me that clean water is not simply a resource—it is the foundation upon which health, education, and innovation are built. Without it, other advances—from clean energy to medical breakthroughs—cannot take root.

Solving this challenge requires more than temporary aid. It calls for sustainable, scalable solutions: solar-powered desalination in coastal communities; decentralized filtration systems that can be maintained locally; education and training programs that create skilled water engineers within the very communities they serve. These solutions require cross-disciplinary thinking, where engineering meets public policy, community leadership, and environmental stewardship.

Clean water is the stepping stone for humanity. Meeting this challenge will not only improve the lives of billions but will also unlock the potential of entire nations to thrive, invent, and contribute to a shared future. For me, this challenge is both an engineering problem and a moral imperative—because when we solve water, we open the floodgates to everything else humanity can achieve.

CHAPTER 16

Elevate Your Style: Mastering the Braided Essay

> ELEVATED WRITING STYLE MEANS TO LEAVE NO DOUBT ABOUT WHO YOU ARE AND WHAT YOU VALUE.

Imagine weaving a friendship bracelet. You pick a few threads, each a different color, and braid them together into something intense and vibrant. A braided essay works the same way. Instead of focusing on one single idea or event, you take two or three seemingly unrelated threads from your life and weave them together into a unified, meaningful story. The result? A creative, dynamic essay that showcases your complexity as a person.

The braided essay is an advanced strategy that requires finesse. But when done well, it can be the kind of essay that sticks in an admissions officer's mind long after they've finished reading.

What Is a Braided Essay?

A braided essay alternates between different storylines or themes, connecting them in unexpected ways. Picture a book where one chapter tells the story of a hero's quest, and the next is a journal entry from a side character that gives you a whole new perspective. By the end, the pieces come together like puzzle pieces, creating a bigger picture.

In your essay, you might:

- Alternate between your passion for baking and your relationship with your grandmother.
- Weave together your love for stargazing and your determination to pursue astrophysics.
- Link a soccer injury with your journey to rediscover resilience.

The key is finding threads that, when braided together, reveal something bigger about you—something a single story might not.

How to Start Your Braided Essay

1. Pick your threads. The first step is identifying two or three ideas, experiences, or themes you want to explore. These threads should:

- Be different enough to feel distinct.
- Have some underlying connection that will reveal itself as you write.

For example:
Thread 1: The first time you performed on stage and felt alive

under the spotlight.

Thread 2: Your struggles with shyness as a child.

Thread 3: A transformative moment when you spoke up for yourself in a class debate.

Together, these threads might tell a story about how you found your voice—literally and figuratively.

2. Structure your essay. Think of your essay like a playlist that alternates between your favorite songs. You'll switch back and forth between the threads, creating rhythm and movement. A simple structure looks like this:

Opening: Begin with a single thread to hook the reader.

Middle sections: Alternate between the threads, moving the stories forward in short sections (a few paragraphs or less).

Closing: Tie the threads together into one unified takeaway.

Pro tip: Use transitions intentionally. Even if your threads seem initially unrelated, a single word, phrase, or idea can subtly connect them. For example:

"Under the spotlight, I finally felt seen." (Thread 1)

"But as a shy kid, I spent years trying to hide." (Thread 2)

3. Focus on moments, not overviews. A braided essay thrives on vivid, specific moments. Instead of telling the reader everything about your shyness or your love of stargazing, show them.

Instead of this: "I've always loved stargazing. It's taught me patience and curiosity."

Try this: "On summer nights, I'd climb onto the roof with a flashlight and a star chart, feeling like I could reach the constellations with my fingertips."

Can you imagine the scenes? The idea is to achieve an essay that feels alive and personal.

4. Bring it all together. The magic of the braided essay is in the way the threads flow into one another. The reader should feel like the different parts of your story were always meant to fit together, even if they didn't see it coming. The consistency of your inner monologue achieves this. The stories are different, but your voice is the same.

For example, suppose your essay weaves together your love of baking and your grandmother's influence. In that case, the conclusion might highlight how those two threads inspired your interest in studying chemistry and developing sustainable food solutions.

Common Pitfalls (and How to Avoid Them)

Pitfall 1: Too many threads. Two or three threads are plenty. More than that, your essay risks becoming confusing.

Pitfall 2: Forcing connections. The essay will be confusing if your threads don't naturally fit together. Choose themes that share an emotional or thematic connection, even if they seem unrelated on the surface.

Pitfall 3: Uneven attention. Don't let one thread dominate. Each one should feel equally important, contributing to the larger story.

Why the Braided Essay Works

A braided essay isn't just a creative exercise; it's a way to show depth. Life isn't linear, and neither are you. By intertwining different parts of your story, you demonstrate how your experiences, passions, and challenges shape who you are.

For example, let's say your essay explores:

- Your love for running (Thread 1)
- The memory of losing a close friend (Thread 2)
- Your efforts to support mental health awareness at school (Thread 3)

At first, these threads might seem disconnected. But by the end, the reader sees how running became a way to process grief and how that loss motivated your advocacy work.

The braided essay is challenging, but also an opportunity to stand out. It shows you're not afraid to take risks or approach a story from a unique angle. So, grab your "threads" and start weaving. Who knows? You might just create something unforgettable.

Let's put this into practice and see how it works.

Braided Essay Example

Thread 1: The Piano Recital

I stood backstage, fingers poised above the keys of my imaginary piano, rehearsing the concerto in my mind. The stage lights were a glaring reminder of the hundreds of eyes waiting beyond the curtain. I could feel the familiar tightening in my chest, a blend of fear and exhilaration. My mother's voice echoed in my head, reminding me to breathe deeply and trust the hours of practice. As the curtain rose, I stepped into the spotlight, each note a testament to discipline and passion.

Thread 2: The Science Fair

My display board stood amid a sea of other projects in the school gymnasium. My experiment on renewable energy sources—a homemade wind turbine—whirred softly, the product of countless evenings spent in the garage. I remembered the initial failures: the blades that wouldn't spin and the motor that refused to generate power. Each setback had been a lesson in perseverance, much like learning a challenging piece on the piano. When the judges approached, I explained my project with the confidence I aimed for in my performances.

Thread 3: The Hiking Trip

High in the mountains, the air was thin and crisp, each breath a reminder of the altitude we had climbed. My father and I paused on the trail, overlooking a valley bathed in the golden light of dawn. The climb had been arduous, marked by moments of doubt and fatigue. Yet, reaching the summit offered a perspective I couldn't find at sea level. It was a reminder that the greatest rewards often come after the toughest climbs whether on a mountain path or a personal journey.

Reflection and Connection

These moments, standing on stage, presenting at the science fair, and summiting a mountain, are more than isolated events. They are interconnected threads that weave through the fabric of my life, each reinforcing the values of resilience, dedication, and passion. The discipline I cultivated in music translates to my academic and extracurricular pursuits, driving me to tackle challenges head-on and embrace the learning process.

Music taught me the importance of practice and patience, skills that proved invaluable during the countless hours in the garage perfecting my science project. Similarly, the perseverance required to reach a mountain summit mirrored the determination needed to see my projects through to completion. These experiences have shaped my approach to life, underscor-

ing the belief that with effort and resilience, I can overcome obstacles and achieve my goals.

Conclusion

As I look toward the future and the opportunities that college presents, I see the continuation of this journey. Each new challenge will be an extension of the lessons I've learned from the piano keys, the science experiments, and the mountain trails. I am ready to embrace these challenges, confident in my ability to weave new threads into the rich tapestry of my life.

Implementation Tips for a Braided Essay

Identify core themes. Choose a few key experiences or themes that reflect your personal growth and values.

Interweave narratives. Alternate between different threads throughout the essay, creating a rhythm and flow that connects each narrative.

Use transitions. Smooth transitions between threads help maintain coherence and guide the reader through your essay.

Reflect and connect. Regularly reflect on the connections among the various threads, identifying common themes and lessons.

Conclude. Bring the threads together in a cohesive conclusion, highlighting how these experiences have collectively prepared you for future challenges and opportunities.

You can create a multidimensional and engaging narrative showcasing your unique experiences and insights using the braided essay technique.

The examples provided are fictional and explicitly created for illustrative purposes to demonstrate how to apply different writing techniques, such as the braided essay style, to a college application essay. They are not taken from real people's essays and are designed to inspire your writing.

Example Customized to Your Experience

To illustrate how you can adapt the braided essay structure to your own experiences, here's a revised version that incorporates placeholders for personal anecdotes:

Thread 1: The Soccer Tournament

I stood on the field, the crowd's roar a distant hum as I focused on the ball at my feet. The championship match was the culmination of months of early morning practices and grueling drills. My coach's advice to "play with heart" echoed in my mind as I dribbled past defenders. Each goal I scored was a testament to teamwork and perseverance.

Thread 2: The Robotics Competition

Our robot stood ready for its final test in the bustling convention center. Countless hours in the lab, troubleshooting code, and refining our design led to this moment. The initial failures—motors that wouldn't turn, sensors that misread data—taught us resilience. When our robot completed the obstacle course flawlessly, it was a testament to the success of collaboration and innovation.

Thread 3: Volunteering at the Shelter

At the community shelter, I served meals to those in need, with each interaction reminding me of the power of kindness. By listening to the stories of the shelter's residents, I learned about resilience in the face of adversity. These moments of connection and empathy shaped my understanding of community and responsibility.

Reflection and Connection

These experiences, on the soccer field, at the robotics competition, and volunteering at the shelter, are more than just activities. They are interwoven threads that define who I am. The discipline of sports drives my academic and extracurricular efforts; the problem-solving skills of robotics fuel my intellectual curiosity; and the empathy I gain from volunteering informs my worldview.

Conclusion

As I prepare for college, I see the continuation of this journey. Each new challenge will extend the lessons learned from the soccer field, the robotics lab, and the community shelter. I am ready to embrace these challenges, confident in my ability to weave new threads into the rich tapestry of my life.

By substituting the placeholders with your own experiences, you can create an essay that is uniquely yours. Remember, the goal is to showcase your individual journey and the qualities that make you a strong candidate for college.

CHAPTER 17

Your Essay Is an Invitation

> SPECIFIC STORIES EVOKE SPECIFIC EMOTIONS, AND IT IS THESE EMOTIONS THAT ADMISSIONS OFFICERS REMEMBER.

As the author of your personal story, you have a responsibility to avoid being bland and generic. Are you the kind of student who begins writing with the goal of constructing a persona from the ground up, thinking, "I want them to think of me as this X kind of person?" This shows great enthusiasm but be cautious; generalizations can undermine your application. Imagine an admissions officer reading hundreds of essays. Each essay tends to blend into the next when students write about being "the kind of person" they think colleges desire. I see numerous essays that start with "Ever since I was a child," or "As far back as I can remember …" Statements like "I have always loved debate competitions" may sound admirable, but they fail to stand out. Why? They lack the personal, specific details that make you unique. Instead of revealing who you are, such statements leave you indistinguishable from countless others.

You be the judge. Read the following statement and analyze it.

I have always loved debate competitions. Not only do I learn while competing, but many of my deepest lessons have come just from spending time with my teammates, delving into deep issues of great significance to society.

At first glance, this passage seems fine. However, upon closer inspection, it appears vague and generic. This could describe anyone who has ever attended a debate competition. It's not about you. The key to a memorable essay is specificity: anecdotes, emotions, and reflections that only you can share.

Think of your essay as an invitation. You are welcoming the reader, and the first two lines serve as a handshake, making a strong first impression. Make them count by directly revealing a pivotal moment in your life. *Begin* with the most intense experience and *skip* the tedious introductions. Instead of stating your love for debate, recount an instance that embodies your passion.

Example:

After we lost the tournament, we had two hours to kill before heading home. My teammates and I stumbled upon a tiny, windowless Chinese restaurant. While slurping wonton soup, we debated mandatory voting. I argued that it enhances liberty because refusing to vote becomes a deliberate political act rather than a sign of laziness. The debate became so animated that we almost missed the bus.

This story is vivid, personal, and uniquely yours. It reveals your passion for debate in a way that no generic statement could.

Of course, no moment is truly powerful and impressive without emotions. Or, as they say, "If it doesn't bleed, it doesn't read."

What did you feel at that moment? Excitement? Frustration? Pride? Your emotional reaction adds depth and connects the reader to your experience.

Example:

The frustration of losing stung, but the debate over wonton soup reignited my love for argument, not to win a trophy, but to uncover new ideas.

Next comes the bigger picture. Tie your story to your broader identity. How does this moment reflect who you are or what you value?

Example:

That night, I realized that debate isn't just about arguments; it's about connection—understanding others' perspectives while sharing my own.

KEY TAKEAWAYS:

- Generic essays blur together; specific essays stand out.

- Use vivid scenes, honest dialogue, emotions, and reflections to create memorable stories.

- Start your essay at a key moment, not at the beginning of time.

- Specificity isn't just about facts; it's about showing how you think, feel, and grow.

CHAPTER 18

Avoiding the Trap of Overemphasizing Accomplishments

> *YOUR MEDALS TELL US WHAT YOU DID.*
> *YOUR STORY TELLS US WHO YOU ARE.*

Accomplishments are impressive, but many of them are also common. Essays that focus solely on victories can feel shallow. Admissions officers are already aware of your accolades from your application.

This one is tough to let go of. By this time in your journey, you may have earned a medal or two, achieved some substantial wins in Speech and Debate, DECA, or your Robotics Club. You have worked hard and might be your school's top dog. But there are fifty states in the union, plus D.C., and several U.S. territories with over 28,727 high schools. That is approximately 2.23 million high school students from the U.S. alone applying to college each year, and among them are many league champions, valedictorians, and debate winners. If you're the best in the country at something, admissions will know it from your application. If you're tempted to show off an accomplishment, pause momentarily. Can you explore the other side? Sometimes, disappointment can be interesting. Notice that one of the new Common App prompts asks about failure. That's a loud message that your trophies are boring.

As I write this, I am reminded of Shelley. She was an accomplished volleyball player, and she came to me with an essay that reflected her skills in that sport. I don't need to reproduce it here because you already know it: a big victory when the chips were down, meaningful moments with teammates, a narrative about the virtues of hard work, perseverance, and sacrifice. She chose her hook carefully, featuring her doing push-ups to illustrate her toughness.

Can you do push-ups? So can the other eight million high school athletes in the country.

Don't write what you think they want to hear. Write what you want to say. Authenticity resonates more than perfection. When we focus on perfection, we lose the emotional connection, and at that point, the essay becomes a narration of events, a series of causes and effects, and a page full of factoids. Only your emotions can create a bond with the reader. So, instead of focusing on her winning game, I advised Shelly to concentrate not on the winning element of the competition but on herself. On who she was despite the win, not because of it.

If you are reading this but are not an athlete, do not give up on this example. Use it to discover who you are and how you can turn your story to your advantage. Ask yourself this question: What is something no one knows about me that I don't talk about? And don't be afraid to be vulnerable.

KEY TAKEAWAYS:

- Your achievements already live on your application—your essay must reveal something deeper.

- Vulnerability and reflection are more powerful than victory speeches.

- Colleges are not impressed by perfection; they are moved by growth and authenticity.

- Focus your essay on who you are becoming, not just what you have achieved.

YOUR TURN: BEGIN WRITING USING THESE PRACTICE PROMPTS

- Describe a moment when you failed and what you learned.

- Write about an argument you've had that changed your perspective.

- Think of a time when you felt deeply connected to others. What caused that connection?

- Answering these prompts in detail will help you uncover the stories that best illustrate who you are.

- **Tip:** Balance achievements with struggles or failures that shaped you.

- A friendly reminder before you start: Trying to be someone you're not often results in clichés.

CHAPTER 19

Digging for Gold: Memorable Writing Balances Logic and Emotion

FACTS INFORM. EMOTIONS TRANSFORM.

When you write with precision, you invite your reader into your world. They see what you see, feel what you feel, and leave with a sense of who you are, not just as a student, but as a person. Remember that the goal of your essay isn't just to tell them what kind of person you are; it's to show them through your stories, emotions, and reflections.

It's easy to get overwhelmed and focus on content, but once you have your draft, stop and reflect: *What kind of feeling are you creating?*

Think of your essay as a movie. What mood do you want your audience to experience? Write it down before you begin: I want to convey a range of emotions, such as suspense, sadness, joy, and hope, and list at least four or five of these emotions. Will the mood in the essay change as you go from zero to hero? If so, plan that ahead of time. At what point will you shift the mood, and how will you do that? Use specific words and shorter sentences to introduce that "staccato" feeling, or opt for longer, more descriptive compound-complex sentences that read slower but are rich with emotion. Whether it's hope, curiosity, or determination, use your words to evoke that feeling. Your sequence of events, emotional highlights, and reflections should all work together to leave the reader with a lasting impression of you.

Crafting a compelling essay is like mining for gold. The golden nuggets of your story lie in the specifics. Don't be afraid to explore moments of failure, confusion, or discovery. These moments, told from your perspective, create the emotional connection to set your voice apart. So, grab your metaphorical pickax and start digging into your experiences. What you uncover might be your ticket to college.

I once had a student who wrote about his efforts to join the swim team. He showed up with his impressive Speedo strapped around his 230-pound frame and splashed vigorously, somehow making it despite everyone's stifled giggles and whispers. By the end of the season, he had become a lean, mean swimming machine, proving to everyone that size doesn't matter, and even earned a school award for it.

Find the courage, struggle, and internal conflict within the situation you're describing. You are the hero of your story, but your decisions, actions, and realizations are viewed through the lens of time and circumstances. Focus on illustrating the emotional growth that comes with both losses and victories. Did you confront your fears?

Did you pursue your dreams? Did you face others to discover yourself in the end? So, write with honesty, not embellishment. Let your words carry the weight of your effort and your quiet victories. Make it easy for your reader to *feel* what was at stake; even if your story is extraordinary, it should still be human.

When colleges ask you to describe a time when you influenced others, whether through leadership, persuasion, friendship, or simply by being present, the main question behind the prompt is: How does your presence impact those around you? Whether you led a team, tutored your younger sibling, helped your family, or changed someone's thinking through your art, admissions officers want to see how your values show up in real-life situations. This essay isn't about telling others what to do. It's about demonstrating what happens when you show up and what that reveals about the kind of influence you'll bring to a college campus.

Here is how one student made the most of his personal story, which earned him multiple acceptances into the Top Ten schools in the country.

Describe an example of how you have positively influenced others.

In my sophomore year, I was diagnosed with prediabetes. At the time, this felt inevitable; I come from generations of bubble guts and beer bellies. However, the bleak outlook frightened me; I had one final chance to change my lifestyle before it was too late.

During winter break, I promised myself to lose weight. I've always viewed obesity as a personal issue, but at first search, I was astounded by how massive the obesity epidemic was: globally, millions of teens like me are obese, bullied, and depressed, just as I was. With a million different diet programs to choose from, I took the "just do them all" approach. I suddenly transitioned to a paleo-keto-low-carb-high-protein-high-fiber-low-fat-probiotic-glorified-anorexic fad diet, and naturally, I failed. I was hopeless but adamant. After learning intermittent fasting and caloric control, I managed macronutrients while eating in a four-hour window. Within eight months, I'd lost 63 pounds and reached a healthy blood sugar. I was fit as a fiddle.

Though I'd achieved fitness myself, it was difficult to watch friends struggle with hiding their body fat as I once did. As a bullying victim, I knew what their insecurity felt like and their astonishment when it took me just four months to undo a decade of pain. So, when two friends asked me how I did it, I knew I could help. We'd all strive for fitness together.

By the first week, I realized the immensity of the task. Motivating myself was much easier than the others since there were no external reminders, but internal motivation drove me forward. To push my friends through hard workouts and strict diets, I created a group chat to help them track macronutrients, calories, and our workouts at Crunch Fitness.

Holding each other accountable became easier and more productive. By the end of the first month, the progress pictures showcased our dedication; we all lost weight, gained muscle, and felt more comfortable with our health.

I was surprised when friends I've helped lose weight started assisting others in doing the same. What began as a necessary intervention to prevent diabetes evolved into a chain reaction of individuals striving to improve themselves.

Let's talk about "optional" essays. Colleges like to make them seem like extra credit, a small side dish you can accept or decline. I

DIGGING FOR GOLD: MEMORABLE WRITING BALANCES LOGIC AND EMOTION

like to think of the optional essays like that final question on a game show that could double your winnings. You don't *have* to answer it, but why leave easy points on the table?

Optional doesn't mean "meh, skip it." In admissions language, optional means, *"Show us if you actually care about this college."* When you write it, you're showing the school you're invested enough to go the extra mile, and you have planned and organized your time to have enough to spare for the "optional." When you don't, you're silently telling them, *"I'm good with the bare minimum."* Guess which message leaves the best impression?

The optional essay is also your bonus round. The rest of your application has fixed sections: GPA, test scores, activities, and a main essay. The optional space is your chance to include something they haven't seen yet: the robotics project you built in your garage, the nonprofit you started over summer, or the reason your sophomore grades look like a rollercoaster. It's the one part where you control the story entirely.

And here's another secret: Many "optional" prompts are sneaky "Why Us?" questions in disguise. They want to see if you've researched their programs, professors, or campus culture. If you skip it, you miss the chance to leave your mark.

(Optional) Duke University seeks a talented, engaged student body that embodies the wide range of human experience; we believe that the diversity of our students makes our community stronger. If you'd like to share a perspective you bring or experiences you've had to help

us understand you better, perhaps related to a community you belong to, your family, or your cultural background, we encourage you to do so. Real people are reading your application, and we want to do our best to understand and appreciate the real people applying to Duke.

The air near the Tapioca Express is heavy with the savory tang of fried pork drifting from the shop next door. My friends and I stand in line for tea, the scent clinging to our jackets. Around us, the air hums with a musical chaos: Mandarin rolling like a string of beads, Hindi curling through the air in lilting rhythms, Tagalog bright and quick, and every so often, an English "Dude!" cutting in like a cymbal crash. Most wouldn't call this mix pleasant—the smell of oil, the chorus of languages, the press of bodies in line, but I love it here.

I head to the library, anticipating the musty comfort of books and the chatter of my Honors Multivariable Calculus class. To bystanders, we might seem like just boisterous kids. But we are more than that: distinct, diverse, yet aware that our hearts beat in the same rhythm.

I wasn't always around diversity like this. My two elementary schools were both predominantly Asian families, but a world apart from the mosaic I live in now. Changing schools felt like crossing into a new country without a map. Surrounded by unfamiliar faces, I thought friendship wasn't in my stars until one day, on the way to French class, the girl walking next to me stopped abruptly as her hijab slipped to her feet. Without thinking, I caught it and handed it back without looking at her hair. I didn't need to see her eyes to know she felt seen and understood. From that day on, I had a friend.

Kafka says, "It is not necessary that you leave the house; remain at your table and listen…The world will present itself to you for its unmasking." My "community"? The nerds, the comedians, the tight-knit best friends, and yes, the Asians. My future isn't bound by the languages I speak —

DIGGING FOR GOLD: MEMORABLE WRITING BALANCES LOGIC AND EMOTION

they're simply tools to cross cultural boundaries and embrace difference in race, faith, and age. Kafka was right; the world has presented itself to me, and I am ready to accept it.

We all have a story, and that's what makes us special. However, often, once the story unfolds on the page and we become engrossed in the feelings, we forget to check the logic behind it all. This can lead to committing logical fallacies that will weaken the argument by exposing gaps in reasoning and distract from the message.

Some prompts are especially tricky and will require diligent checkpoints to ensure the logic is sound and that you are not getting tangled up in words. The University of Chicago is notorious for asking current students to write them, and many of these prompts sound more like multilayered riddles and academic challenges than actual writing prompts. I recall prompts from the past that were truly panic-inducing, such as:

- "What is so odd about odd numbers?"
- "Find x."
- "Where is Waldo, really?"
- "You are on Mars, and there is no way out."

Your job is not to impress with facts, but to show how you think, especially when no one tells you the rules of the game. Here is an example of how a student approached an equally challenging prompt:

Suppose there's a limited amount of matter in the universe. How can Olive Garden (along with other restaurants and their concepts of food infinity) offer truly unlimited soup, salad, and breadsticks? Explain this using any method of analysis you wish—physics, biology, economics, history, theology ... the options, as you can tell, are endless. (Max 650 words)

Infinity is often used in mathematics to express an abstract, unattainable, and undefined value. Yet, several restaurants keep infinity at the core of their business model.

Olive Garden's advertisement serves the purpose of associating Olive Garden with the term unlimited. While other restaurant chains focus on diversifying their advertisements to showcase potential new items or locations, Olive Garden consistently ensures that its unlimited concept of soup, salad, and breadsticks is clearly articulated to the average consumer. Advertising's main job is to effectively convince the average consumer to be intrigued by their product. The psychology of the consumer is to want the "best bang for the buck." Thus, one of the appealing tactics that Olive Garden applies is the affordability of its unlimited deal. Therefore, their customer retention rate remains positive because the main reason why consumers come never changes.

The existence of buffets like Sweet Tomatoes thrives on a similar model that embodies the concept of infinity. Customers pay a one-time price and gain access to various entrees with the option to eat as much as they desire. The concept of buffets was formalized by the Swedish and the French. While the Swedish provided buffets at a much lower cost, the French elevated them to a more lavish experience. The versatility of buffets to appeal to different financial backgrounds ensures that the idea of food infinity is inclusive of everyone, allowing the concept to remain endless.

Food infinity benefits restaurants as well. With the buffet style, the costs associated with employing waitstaff are eliminated since consumers serve themselves. Additionally, the volume of customers entering and leaving the restaurant significantly exceeds that of sit-down establishments. The average diner spends considerably more time at a traditional sit-down restaurant than at buffets. The increase in these profit margins allows buffets to sustain the concept of food infinity.

It is a human tendency to debunk and disregard irrational and abstract ideas, as we often prefer to cling to things that appeal to us on a logical or emotional level. The brilliance of buffets lies in their ability to satisfy both. From both a consumer and a restaurant perspective, they prove to be advantageous, as these establishments reduce costs that typical restaurants must incur. For consumers, buffets provide the best value for their money, which is the central desire of every buyer. Emotionally, the entertainment associated with the unique experience created in a buffet setting makes it a favored dining choice. While true infinity is unattainable, its underlying concept remains the foundation for exhilaration, enjoyment, and eccentricity.

Yet maybe restaurants like Olive Garden and Sweet Tomatoes are capitalizing on a reality no one knows. To this day, astronomers have not reached conclusive evidence that the universe is finite or infinite. Research indicates that our observable universe is limited to approximately 46 billion light-years in all directions. That leaves an immense possibility that matter continues to exist, and we'll forever be unaware of it. It raises the question of whether matter truly is limited in the universe. Therefore, the hypothesis presented in the prompt has not been proven, which supports the theoretical possibility of these restaurants offering unlimited food. The Big Bang may be considered the reason for the birth of our universe, but it's never credited for the birth of the entirety of space and time.

Before this, the universe was undergoing cosmic inflation, filled with matter, radiation, and expansion, and creating new space at an exponential rate. Therefore, while logically, we believe matter to be finite until definite proof is shown, which studies indicate is practically impossible for *humans to discover, restaurants with food at the center of their business model can never fail just because of "limited" matter.*

The essays shared here, though written by different students, all follow what I call the 5 "P's" strategy of good college essay writing.

Personal: Your essay should be based on your real life. This isn't a place for fiction or imaginary "what if" scenarios. Every story and detail must be grounded in your actual experiences, no matter how minor they seem.

Purpose: Your story needs a "why" behind it. Why does it matter to you? Why should it matter to the reader? Purpose provides your essay with direction so you're not wandering through paragraphs without a point.

Plot twist: A plot twist in your essay isn't just about surprising the reader; it's about delivering an unexpected shift in meaning or perspective that redefines the entire piece. In comedy, that is the punchline which flips the setup in a way that gets a reaction. In storytelling, a plot twist does the same thing: it takes the reader somewhere they didn't think they were going, yet makes perfect sense in hindsight. In your personal statement, this might be the moment when your story turns from struggle to insight, from an ordinary experience to an extraordinary realization. This is where your essay sticks in the reader's mind, and they think, *I didn't see that coming, but now it all clicks.*

Proof: Don't just say you're hardworking, resilient, or curious, show it. Use specific examples, vivid moments, and sensory details from your life to prove it. The more concrete the evidence, the more memorable the essay. Show how *your* experiences shape your view of the world. The same event might happen to a hundred people, but your perspective makes it different.

Polishing: A strong essay is not just about what you say, it's about how you say it. Edit for clarity, remove unnecessary words, and ensure every sentence has purpose. A well-polished piece demonstrates effort and pride in your work.

Whether your essay is 250 words or 650, you need to begin with a strong hook. This typically consists of one or two sentences with a single purpose: to capture the reader's attention and keep it. A captivating first sentence doesn't start with dull facts or safe statements but with a shock, such as an anecdote, contradiction, sensory detail, question, or contrast. It introduces a disturbance, tension, conflict, or question that draws the reader in. Your words should evoke curiosity or urgency, so they feel compelled to keep reading to learn more.

Anecdotal Openings

The fire alarm went off during my SAT, and I didn't move.

Admissions officer note: Immediate tension. I'm asking why you stayed.

The day I failed my American History final, I learned how to win debates.

Admissions officer note: The contradiction hooks me; I want to know how failure led to an unexpected skill.

Contradicting Statement Openings

I don't believe in the "finding your passion" statement.

Admissions officer note: This student is challenging a cliché. Makes me curious about your worldview.

I lied to my grandmother the day before she died.

Admissions officer note: Emotional risk-taking; this will either fall flat or will be unforgettable.

I've never been the smartest person in the room, and I plan to keep it that way.

Admissions officer note: This student subverts expectations. This student understands humility and collaboration.

Vivid Sensory Detail Openings

The scent of lavender and bleach will forever remind me of home.

Admissions officer note: Strong sensory anchor; I can picture, smell, and feel your world instantly.

I still hear the door slam, followed by my parents' last arguments.

Admissions office note: This is a strong tie of a physical sound to an emotional state; very human.

Early morning coffee tastes different when you are running late for the DECA competition.

Admissions officer note: Poetic, mysterious. I'm interested in finding out the backstory.

Thought-Provoking Openings

What do you do when the thing you love starts to hate you back?

Admissions officer note: Dramatic metaphor; a great hint to the student's journey from burnout to self-discovery.

If you could trade your life for someone else's for a day, would you? I did.

Admissions officer note: This is action-packed and introspective at the same time.

What if "good enough" was never the goal?

Admissions officer note: Signals ambition or perfectionism; kept me curious.

Juxtaposition / Contrast Opening

I learned more about leadership from babysitting a toddler than from my student government advisor.

Admissions officer note: Humor and humility are a great combination.

Two computer programmers raised me, but I still don't understand how Wi-Fi works.

Admissions officer note: Relatable self-deprecation; helped me to connect instantly.

KEY TAKEAWAYS:

- Specific details ground the story; emotional reflections elevate it.

- Decide in advance what feeling you want to leave the reader with, such as hope, curiosity, or determination.

- Control the pacing and mood through sentence structure and word choice.

- Explore failure, confusion, discovery, all those moments that can create real emotional bonds.

CHAPTER 20

Words Matter: Visual Language

> "STUDENTS WHO SHARE VERY LITTLE ABOUT THEMSELVES MAKE A SIGNIFICANT MISTAKE IN THEIR ESSAYS. EVEN IF THE ESSAY IS WELL-WRITTEN, ONE THAT LACKS A PERSONAL TOUCH CANNOT SUCCEED."
> — ADMISSIONS COUNSELOR, LOYOLA MARYMOUNT UNIVERSITY

An anecdote is a brief retelling of a memorable event or experience. In your essay, anecdotes can be used as an effective introduction and add some personality to your writing. A picture is worth a thousand words, but is it possible that using visual language can be worth a thousand pictures? Guide your readers using figurative language and with words that convey emotion and meaning. Express everything as simply as you can. Don't forget your reader! In this case, the reader is the *admissions* officer, but don't allow that to intimidate you. The same emotions drive all human beings, and all humans seek happiness.

Read how one high school student approached the problem and how he was successfully able to use visuals in his own words:

> I spent days and weeks thinking about what to write. I wanted something compelling enough to become the topic of perhaps the single most important 649 words of my life so far. After a dozen or more false starts, I thought of sea cucumbers.
>
> This became one sentence, then two, and I finished the bulk of it in a single afternoon. Unlike any of my other essays, it felt almost effortless. I thought that it really revealed personality and required very little revision from the first draft to the final version.

Here's an excerpt:

Some people are born brave. I wasn't one of the lucky ones. Any creepy crawlies within my line of sight meant immediate temporary paralysis, a profound panic attack, and a fight-or-flight response sprint in a random direction lasting no less than ten seconds. This summer, I had to confront my worst fears daily as they manifested themselves in the physical form underneath the mud of the South Florida coast.

Stepping into the sulfurous mass that swirled and pulsed with movements of mysterious mud-denizens, I surrendered my socks and sneakers to the marsh gods in the name of climate research. Gingerly, at first, I stuck my hands into the depths in search of the tiny sea cucumbers, the main food source of the whooping crane and the subject of my EarthWatch research.

"Fear is a mind-killer," I repeated, recalling the quote from Frank Herbert's Dune, one of my favorite sci-fi works, hoping that the words would calm my mind as my consciousness developed elaborate escape plans. Ladders, a rooftop, a boat, and a swim, perhaps a plane and a parachute. Was there a way out of here that did not end with an ambulance ride? "Hannah, catch those sea cucumbers," my professor ordered in his Southern drawl, arousing me from my daydreams. Alas, I was still in Florida, wearing a bucket hat and sporting mosquito bites on my legs. I was afraid to die, not from the possibility of not making a catch but from catching the wrong specimen. I was afraid of the infamous mud snake—a species of nonvenomous semi-aquatic beady-eyed creature.

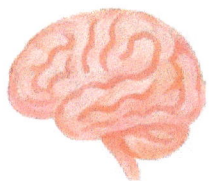

Now it is your turn:

1. Reflect on your personal connection to the college or program. What initially attracted you to this university? (Was it the location, a campus visit, an online webinar, or a specific program?)

2. What aspects of the university's culture or values resonate with you? (For example, its diversity, innovation, creativity, or community spirit.)

3. How does this university's setting (urban/rural/global) inspire or fit your personality, values, or interests? (E.g., the energy of New York City or the collaborative nature of a close-knit college town.)

4. What are your long-term academic interests and goals? What specific educational programs, majors, or departments at this school align with your goals? How will this school help you achieve them?

5. Why are you passionate about this subject? (What personal experiences or intellectual curiosities have led to this interest?)

6. Have you researched professors, research centers, or unique courses?

7. Which ones excite you the most, and why? How does their work or teaching connect to your interests? (For example: "Dr. Thomas Wisniewski's paper on localized proteomics inspired me to pursue Alzheimer's research.")

8. What unanswered questions do you want to explore in your chosen field?

9. How will this school's resources help you answer those questions?

10. Are there extracurricular opportunities or programs at this school that excite you? (E.g., clubs, symposiums, events, or conferences like the Joint Neuroscience Colloquia.)

11. Why are these opportunities meaningful to you?

12. How will you contribute to the school's community? What unique perspective, skills, or experiences will you bring? (For

example, if you're a jazz musician, will you join music clubs or integrate music into research?)

13. How do your hobbies or passions align with the school's culture? (For example, if the school values innovation, how have you demonstrated creative problem-solving or new ideas?)

14. What personal experiences have influenced your academic or extracurricular goals? Did you have a defining moment (like volunteering, a research project, or a class) that solidified your interests?

15. What questions or challenges arose from those experiences that you want to explore further? How has your background, community, or values shaped your goals for college? (For example, if you volunteered with Alzheimer's patients, how did that connect to your interest in neuroscience?)

16. What makes this school different from others? What resources (labs, research opportunities, faculty, study abroad, or events) excite you most? How are these resources uniquely suited to your academic and personal interests?

17. Which professors, mentors, or research centers do you hope to work with? Why? What about their work inspires you?

18. What campus events, traditions, or student organizations do you see yourself participating in? (E.g., Computer Numerical Control symposiums, hackathons, entrepreneurship competitions.)

19. How does the school's approach to education (e.g., "without walls" learning at NYU) inspire you?

20. Why do you believe you belong at this school? What values, qualities, or attributes do you share with the student community? (For example: "At NYU, I see a home for misfits, abstract thinkers, and visionaries, people like me.")

21. How will you contribute to the university's mission or culture? What unique skills, perspectives, or experiences will you share? What specific goals do you want to achieve while at this school? Think about academic, personal, and extracurricular goals.

22. How can you weave a unique or thematic story into your essay? Is there a metaphor (like the one used earlier of jazz for NYU) that ties your interests, values, and the college's offerings together?

23. How can you make the introduction creative, personal, and reflective of who you are? Are you using concrete examples of experiences, opportunities, and goals instead of vague statements? What unique perspective, skills, or experiences will you bring? (For example, if you're a jazz musician, will you join music clubs or integrate music into research?)

24. What unique perspective, skills, or experiences will you bring?

CHAPTER 21

Make Me Feel It: The Science Behind Showing, Not Telling

> READERS CONNECT TO ACTION AND EMOTION, AND THAT'S THE KEY TO PULLING THEM INTO YOUR STORY.

Imagine if a college admissions officer had to understand your entire identity through a single scene: thirty seconds of your life captured in a moment and described in a paragraph. Would they see a trophy ceremony, or would they catch you helping your little brother tie his shoes before your first debate tournament? One reveals; the other demonstrates.

"Show don't tell" isn't just a writing rule. Neuroscientists have found that this is a brain rule: When we read sensory-rich storytelling, our brains activate the same regions involved in real-life experiences. You write about a blistering summer track meet, and the reader's body temperature rises. Describe the scent of your grandfather's garage, and their olfactory cortex lights up. When you show, you don't just inform; you recreate.

You could say, "Sarah was sad." Or you could say: "Sarah slumped into the armchair; the letter still crumpled in her hand. Her eyes traced the same raindrop sliding down the window, over and over."

One version tells you what happened. The other lets you feel it. Great writing triggers empathy.

Let's try a few:

Tell: I'm a great piano player.

Show: I mastered Gershwin's *Preludes* for my senior recital, even the final movement, which kept me up three nights in a row.

Tell: I'm a responsible employee.

Show: After three weeks on the job, I was promoted to assistant produce manager and put in charge of three employees, including one who was older than me.

Tell: Traveling changed me.

Show: In Hanoi, I ate crickets from a market stall and haggled for sandals in broken Vietnamese. I didn't just visit, but I put in the effort and adapted.

The sensory activation process is like the whetstone in a writer's toolkit. If you want to show well, lean on four key techniques:

1. **Sensory details.** Describe not just what something looks like, but how it sounds, smells, feels, or tastes. Sensory input builds layers in your imagination.

2. **Micro-actions.** Show the way a character behaves under stress or excitement: tapping their foot, swallowing hard, squinting their eyes, twisting a napkin, clutching a dollar bill, the small stuff that reveals the unspoken.

3. **Internal monologue.** Let the reader in. What is the voice in your head repeating? What do you fear will happen? What do you *wish* you could say but you don't?

4. **Specificity:** Don't write, "a lot of people." Write, "a crowd of high school sophomores in red polos sitting on the bleachers, clutching tight a 'Welcome back, Coach!' banner."

The Adjective Trap (and How to Escape It)

Most students begin brainstorming with a list of adjectives, such as hardworking, curious, empathetic, and friendly. These are fine qualities, but they fall flat unless proven.

Try this instead:
1. Ask three people to list five adjectives they would use to describe you.
2. Highlight the ones that repeat.
3. Choose your top three, then write a story where you never say the word, but the trait becomes clear.

If your word is "resilient," show the moment you trained for a

10K alone after your track team was cut. If it's "resourceful," show how you redesigned the school's club website using free tools when your team lost funding.

Ask a friend or a family member to read and ask them to guess what adjectives you were aiming for. If they get close, you nailed it.

And if all else fails, you can always try to find inspiration in the classics. Let your imagination travel from Hogwarts to Harvard and feel motivated to write like a novelist while still sounding like yourself. After all, great storytelling isn't just for fiction; you can learn from it, borrow the brilliance of novelists, and apply it to your own life experiences.

Here is a snippet from J.K. Rowling's work to inspire your college essay. This is from *Harry Potter and the Philosopher's Stone*:

> A giant of a man was standing in the doorway. His face was almost completely hidden by a long, shaggy mane of hair and a wild, tangled beard, but you could make out his eyes, glinting like black beetles under all the hair.

Let's apply the same colorful technique to a college essay:

> He towered over the rest of the robotics team, six-foot-three with shoulders like a fridge, and didn't say much unless something caught fire. But when our code failed five minutes before the tournament, it was Jacob who pulled out a granola bar, passed it to me, and said, "We'll fix it." That was leadership I hadn't expected.

Let's try one more from Harper Lee's *How to Kill a Mockingbird*:

> Somehow, it was hotter then: a black dog suffered on a summer's

day; bony mules hitched to Hoover carts flicked flies in the sweltering shade of the live oaks on the square.

Let's reimagine this as a description in a college essay and rewrite it:

The gym felt like it was breathing out fire, ceiling fans spun hopelessly above, while my shirt clung to my back, and the whistle around my neck burned against my chest. I'd volunteered to coach the elementary league, thinking it would be fun. It wasn't. The kids' chatter and the heat made my head spin, but I stayed because those second graders thought I was the real deal.

You don't need to sound like Harper Lee. But you *do* need to make your reader feel the heat (or another sensation), whether it's from a summer track meet or a kitchen argument with your dad.

Inspiration is all around us, and we can draw on classics and great writers to use our imagination, and then use our modern voice to capture those moments in our lives that are worth remembering. *The auto shop wasn't just rusted lockers, buzzing fluorescents, and the faint smell of gas that never left my clothes. But when I got the carburetor to fire on my first try, Mr. Franco gave a nod so small you'd miss it if you weren't waiting your whole life for it.*

Showing makes the reader a witness, and a witness remembers the scene. One moment of vivid, specific storytelling is worth more than any summary of traits. Make them feel it. That's what they'll carry with them when they vote yes.

KEY TAKEAWAYS:

- "Show, don't tell" activates the brain and builds emotional resonance.

- Use sensory details, internal monologue, and specific actions to create vivid scenes.

- Make your reader see, hear, and remember the real-life moments. That's the secret to standing out.

CHAPTER 22

What Is a Personality Score?

> "PERSONALITY ISN'T EXTRA; IT'S ESSENTIAL."
> — ADMISSIONS OFFICER, BROWN UNIVERSITY

Even if you haven't seen what the application looks like, once you start writing your essay and filling out the sections of the application, you will understand the straightforward task at hand. However, the process has many pitfalls and hidden nooks and crannies. Here is a little-known fact: Colleges evaluate your personality. How? That is their proprietary secret sauce.

Nevertheless, reviewing former students' applications, as assessed by Admissions, and reading the notes on these applications has provided us with all the necessary information. On many occasions, my students have received a handwritten note on their acceptance letter praising the quality of the student's personal statement, giving us a clue to their essay structure preferences. Some insight into how colleges evaluate applicants can be gleaned from student files, documents that, in some instances, students are permitted to access after acceptance. I've reviewed these files with students, and what stands out is how subjective some of the notes can be. There's also broader speculation about how this subjectivity plays out, especially following the infamous Students for Fair Admissions v. President and Fellows of Harvard College lawsuit filed in 2014 that challenged Harvard's use of race in admissions, claiming that the university discriminated against Asian American applicants by giving them lower personal ratings.

I have dedicated my life to researching and digging into the *why, how,* and *what* this process involves. In many cases, students targeting similar college majors or students who share the same demographics also share almost identical profiles, from the number of AP classes they take to the robotics club and math competitions. This can make each application similar to the next, with the only difference being the personal statement essay. So, when figuring out what colleges want from an applicant, you won't need to look beyond the prompts. Every hint of what colleges are looking for can be found in the prompts, so we can safely summarize the qualities that make an impressive application.

By no means is this an exhaustive list, but here are some of the qualities the admissions have penciled down on the application(s) after a two-member review:

- Displays creative and original thought
- Shows motivation
- Shows self-confidence and takes initiative boldly
- Spirit of independence

- Great intellectual promise
- Substantial academic achievements and disciplined work habits
- Demonstrates genuine curiosity
- Demonstrates maturity
- Natural born leader
- Demonstrates integrity
- Resilience and reaction to setbacks
- Concern for others

What activities and experiences can you write about that highlight one or more of these? How can you demonstrate (rather than just mention) in your essay that you possess these qualities? Will your letters of recommendation (or the LORD, as I call them to emphasize their importance) reflect the same attributes and align well with the activities and achievements you are showcasing? Suppose you are an active Type A personality who participates in student council and helps organize events. In that case, you will also be an outspoken and engaged participant during AP Language class discussions. When your English teacher writes the LORD, this specific proactive and outspoken personality trait will support your application story.

Similarly, a water polo captain will most likely ask the coach for a letter of recommendation and receive a stellar endorsement for consistently showing up and being in the thick of the game.

Next, of course, comes your GPA, and finally, your targeted list of schools. If most of your high school career has been dedicated to being the star of DECA or playing the cello, you should surely target schools that can offer that continuation.

Your narrative should be powerful enough to inspire your reader to reflect on your strengths and personal challenges. Better yet, it should make them remember and think about you. It should be an experience for them as much as it is for you.

To ensure a comprehensive and compelling college application devoid of gaps and red flags, let's approach it systematically:

1. Begin with your history. Reflect on your life's journey, starting from your earliest memory and progressing chronologically. Document significant events and experiences leading up to the present moment. Don't focus solely on the dramatic or life-altering moments; instead, explore the nuances of your personal growth and evolution. Dedicate ample attention to recent years, as they provide a clearer reflection of your current identity and aspirations.

2. Highlight your achievements and accomplishments, but only in the allocated Activities Section. Enumerate any accolades or commendations you've earned, whether academic, extracurricular, or personal milestones. This section serves as a testament to your dedication and resilience. Whether it's sports, community involvement, artistic endeavors, or technological interests, take a moment to reflect on the motivations behind your participation. *Why did you start these activities, and what motivates your ongoing involvement?* Discover experiences that may not have received adequate attention elsewhere in your application, enabling a comprehensive portrayal of your interests and passions.

3. Identify the major influences in your life. Compile a list of individuals, events, artistic works, literature, and music that have left a lasting impression on you. Reflect on how these influences have shaped your worldview, values, and aspirations. This inventory offers insights into your intellectual curiosity and capacity for introspection.

4. **Assess your skills.** Evaluate your competencies and attributes, seeking input from friends and family members if needed. These skills may encompass tangible abilities acquired through learning and practice as well as intangible qualities like leadership or adaptability. Embrace a holistic perspective that encompasses technical proficiencies and personal strengths.

5. **Uncover your passions and aspirations.** Identify the subjects, causes, or activities that ignite your enthusiasm and stir your emotions. Whether it's a sports team, a cherished book, or a pressing societal issue, delve into what resonates deeply with you. Revisit themes mentioned elsewhere in your application, providing a fresh perspective that underscores your authentic passions and convictions.

Use the space below to jot down your ideas.

By carefully addressing each of these aspects, you'll create an application that not only highlights your academic strengths but also provides a well-rounded view of your character, interests, and goals. Take the chance to present an honest and meaningful story that truly reflects who you are.

_____
_____
_____
_____
_____
_____
_____
_____

THE PLOT TWIST IS YOU

CHAPTER 23

Demonstrating Interest from the Start

> INTEREST ISN'T JUST A CHECKBOX; IT'S A SIGNAL, AND COLLEGES ARE MONITORING FROM THE FIRST CLICK TO THE FINAL DECISION.

Admissions counselors rank demonstrated interest as an increasingly decisive factor. Even if the college doesn't have any supplemental essays or a school-specific prompts, you can use the Common Application's topic to indicate your interest in attending a particular school. If this is your plan, it's essential that you do your homework.

Here are a couple of ideas:

Research your intended major. If you're applying to a school that has achieved recognition for that major, or if your major is rare and only a few schools offer it, you've got a good place to start. **Check the courses offered through your major's department and the list of professors who teach them.** On many sites, the professors' recent publications, research, and specific areas of interest will be listed. What appeals to you? Why do you want to study with one or more of these professors? Are there research opportunities you would like to get involved in? These details can demonstrate your interest in attending.

Another suggestion that will prove very useful is to check the mission statement of each college to understand how well you align with the school. Grinnell College, for example, states in part that it "aims to graduate women and men who can think clearly, who can speak and write persuasively and even eloquently, who can evaluate critically both their own and others' ideas, who can acquire new knowledge, and who are prepared in life and work to use their knowledge and their abilities to serve the common good." Students who are compelled to work in the service of the common good could write about how their goals align with those of the university.

CHAPTER 24

Tilt the Odds

> IN A RIGGED GAME, STRATEGY ISN'T OPTIONAL; IT'S SURVIVAL.

The house (colleges) claims to be meritocratic, but its roulette wheel favors certain outcomes. The ball (your application) doesn't land where it "should"; it lands where the tilt, timing, and tactics influence it. Admissions readers sift through thousands of essays. They aren't searching for brilliance; they're seeking pattern disruption. Your true advantage is to break the rhythm with a voice that sounds nothing like the "model student." The goal isn't perfection but connection. You want to make them say: "This kid sounds like someone I would like to meet."

But connection alone isn't enough; you also need to position yourself strategically. Don't just apply where the numbers indicate you are a perfect match but apply where your profile addresses the school's needs. A male student applying to a liberal arts college that is mostly female can give you a slight advantage. Applying to an underenrolled major (like linguistics or classics) is another point in your favor. Another lesser-known benefit can come from targeting schools where your high school is underrepresented.

Even the timing of your application submission can influence the outcome. Some schools offer multiple rounds of admission, such as Early Decision (ED), which allows applicants to apply as early as November and commit if accepted, and Early Action (EA), which enables applying early to receive results sooner without committing if accepted. Therefore, it's important to carefully plan your applications to maximize these opportunities. While you can't control who reviews your applications or when, you can control how early you submit. Apply EA if your junior year grades are strong; this can work in your favor. Applying EA can be advantageous in many cases. If your junior year grades are solid, you may be a good candidate. But if your grades are inconsistent, it might be better to avoid competing against strong EA applicants and instead choose Regular Decision. Focus on working hard during the first semester of your senior year and submit your mid-semester grades to the Regular Decision cycle. This approach helps you avoid the risk of being waitlisted, which often leads to rejections around April.

And when it comes to the essay, don't just answer the prompt; reimagine it. Most students respond to questions like, "What makes you proud?" with safe, expected answers. But what if you wrote why pride scared you until you earned it! Flip the emotional axis. That's the lean of the table. That's where the reader stops and feels.

It's not about luck. It's about reading the lean. Like the worn-out carpet under the roulette table, the college admissions process is riddled with invisible angles. Most students are too busy polishing their résumés to notice. The ones who win? They observe, calculate, and place the bet when the odds whisper, not shout. And that, my dear reader, could be you.

ABOUT THE AUTHOR

Ava Mariya Gencheva is an educator, college admissions consultant, and author with over twenty years of experience helping students craft their stories and gain acceptance to top universities like Harvard, Stanford, and Oxford.

As the founder of VoicED Academy, Ava combines strategic storytelling with insider admissions expertise to help students stand out in a competitive environment. Her students have started companies, created award-winning films, conducted groundbreaking research, and published books while still in high school or college.

In addition to guiding college applicants, Ava writes children's books and organizes youth TED-style talks, giving students a platform to share their voices on stage. Even on weekends, she can be found deep in discussion, often planning the next student event—whether it's a talk, a workshop, or a stage presentation—that challenges young people to think and speak with confidence.

She brings the same passion to curating these experiences as she does to helping students craft essays that can change the course of their lives.

Ava believes that an unforgettable essay isn't just well-written, but also personal, purposeful, and rooted in the writer's authentic voice. And if you ever sit across from her at a table, she'll likely lean in and say, "Your story matters, so let's make it unforgettable."

ADMISSIBILITY CHECKLIST

(For final draft self-audit before you hit submit.)

1. Narrative Clarity

☐ My essay answers the prompt.
- Admissions office note: If you dodge the question, I can't advocate for you in committee.

☐ My central theme is evident in the first 1–2 paragraphs.
- Admissions office note: We read fast; if I don't "get" your essay early, your impact drops.

☐ My essay tells one story, not many stories.
- Admissions officer note: Overcrowded essays dilute your brand.

2. Personal Depth

☐ I reveal something about my character and values.
- Admissions office note: Facts alone don't get you admitted, but your *why* does.

☐ The essay shows—not just tells—my qualities.
- Admissions officer note: "I am resilient" means little without proof through action.

☐ The admissions reader could imagine me on campus from this essay.
- Admissions officer note: If I can't "see" you at our school, I won't advocate for you.

3. Originality & Voice

☐ The essay could only be written by me.
- Admissions officer note: If I could swap your name with another applicant's, the essay is generic and forgettable.

☐ The voice feels natural, not like I'm "performing" for admissions.
- Admissions officer note: Overly formal essays feel robotic.

☐ I stayed away from cliché life lessons, and I have a unique twist.
- Admissions officer note: Learning teamwork is fine, but learning teamwork in a mountain survival trip is memorable.

4. Technical Quality

☐ My grammar, punctuation, and spelling are correct.
- Admissions officer note: Sloppy mechanics is a sloppy work ethic in our eyes.

☐ Sentences vary in length and rhythm.
- Admissions officer note: Monotone writing makes even great stories boring.

☐ I've removed filler words and vague statements.
- Admissions officer note: Every sentence should earn its place.

5. Strategic Fit

☐ This essay complements, not repeats, my activities list.
- Admissions officer note: If you duplicate, you waste a chance to add dimension.

☐ The essay leaves the reader wanting to know more about me.
- Admissions officer note: My job is to advocate for you; give me a reason to do so.

ADMISSIBILITY APPENDIX: Your Final Plot Twist

(Read this before you close the book; it could change your ending.)

Admissions officers are not gatekeepers guarding a secret club; they are readers curious about your story. Your job? Give them one.

1. The Core Checklist

- **Academics:** GPA meets or exceeds the middle 50% range for your target schools—rigor in coursework, AP, IB, or Honors in core subjects.

- **Testing (if applicable):** SAT/ACT scores within the competitive range, or strong alternative demonstrations of skill (subject tests, dual-enrollment grades, portfolios).

- **Extracurriculars Depth:** At least one sustained, high-impact commitment and leadership role, original project, or significant community contribution.

- **Essay Readiness:** Personal statement and supplements are authentic, voice-driven, and strategically aligned to your strengths.

- ❑ **Recommendations:** Strong letters from teachers who know your work ethic and growth.

2. Self-Score Reality Check

Rank yourself **1–3** for each category above:

3: I could not be stronger here.
2: Solid, but there's room for tightening or refining.
1: Needs major work before application submission.

Look at your 1's and 3's; these are your *plot holes*. Fix them before you hit submit.

3. The Final 10-Day Countdown

- ❑ **Days 10–8:** Read your essays aloud. Fix every sentence that doesn't sound like you.

- ❑ **Days 7–5:** Triple-check dates, deadlines, and requirements for each school.

- ❑ **Days 4–3:** Re-confirm recommenders have submitted.

- ❑ **Days 2:** Review your activities list—is every entry purposeful?

- ❑ **Day 1:** Print the whole application. Read it as if you're the admissions officer. Would you admit you?

4. The "If You're Missing This" Rescue Guide

- [ ] Leadership gap? Take the lead by managing a small, fast-paced project like an event, fundraiser, or team initiative before deadlines.

- [ ] Test score concern. Highlight coursework rigor, relevant awards, or self-driven academic work.

- [ ] No "big hook"? Lean hard into depth, reflection, and the story only you can tell.

5. Reality Check Questions

- [ ] Does my application feel like *me* in every section?

- [ ] Will the reader see growth, direction, and purpose?

- [ ] Have I eliminated anything that could confuse, bore, or dilute my impact?

Final Note:

When they finish reading, the admissions committee should feel the way you do when you finish reading a memorable story: changed, moved, impressed, or curious.

ACKNOWLEDGMENTS

This book would not have come to life without the contributions, guidance, and encouragement of many remarkable people.

To my students, past and present, thank you for lending me your stories, your trust, and your willingness to explore the deeper questions. You are the reason I do this work, and every page of this book carries your fingerprints.

To the parents who have invited me to walk alongside their children's journeys, I am honored by your trust. Your belief in both my guidance and their potential has been the foundation of everything I teach and write.

To my husband and children, thank you for your patience, humor, and love through countless late nights, early mornings, and endless edits. You remind me every day that while writing is a solitary act, living the story is never done alone.

To Eric Hübler, whose sharp eye and thoughtful edits strengthened every chapter, and to David Provolo, whose design gave the book its visual voice, I am grateful for your skill, care, and collaboration.

And to every friend, colleague, and reader who offered insight, encouragement, or simply reminded me to keep going, thank you for helping me turn the pages toward this moment.

www.ingramcontent.com/pod-product-compliance
Lightning Source LLC
Chambersburg PA
CBHW070535090426
42735CB00013B/2987